BECKY LUCAS is a comedian who has spent years writing on TV shows and performing stand-up comedy. She has hosted the 2021 Oxfam Gala for the opening night of the Melbourne International Comedy Festival, appeared on *Last One Laughing* on Amazon Prime, performed at the prestigious Just for Laughs festival in Montreal and made her US TV debut on *Conan* – the first Australian woman to perform stand-up comedy on the show. She was a writer on Josh Thomas's Emmy-nominated show *Please Like Me* and has also written sketches for Comedy Central and ABC. And now, if it's okay with everyone, she's decided to write a book.

ACKNOWLEDGMENTS

ACKNOWLEDGMENTS

BECKY LUCAS

A MEMOIR SO FAR

HarperCollinsPublishers

Publisher's note:

The names and identifying details of some people in this book have been changed.

HarperCollins*Publishers*
Australia • Brazil • Canada • France • Germany • Holland • Hungary
India • Italy • Japan • Mexico • New Zealand • Poland • Spain • Sweden
Switzerland • United Kingdom • United States of America

First published in Australia in 2021
by HarperCollins*Publishers* Australia Pty Limited
Level 13, 201 Elizabeth Street, Sydney NSW 2000
ABN 36 009 913 517
harpercollins.com.au

A catalogue record for this book is available from the National Library of Australia.

ISBN 978 1 4607 6147 2 (paperback)
ISBN 978 1 4607 1329 7 (ebook)
ISBN 978 1 4607 8844 8 (audiobook)

Cover and internal design by Andy Warren, HarperCollins Design Studio
Cover photo of Becky Lucas by Anna Hay
Typeset in Baskerville by Kelli Lonergan

Printed and bound by CPI Group (UK) Ltd, Croydon, CR0 4YY

To my friends and family.
I'm sorry for being such a little bitch all the time.
I really love you.

CONTENTS

I'd like to start the book by saying a few thankyous ...

David

I met David in a hostel in Brazil in my early twenties, during the trip of a lifetime. He was American and at first I was grossed out by him. He didn't fit into what I considered my general 'type' – not that I was old enough to have a 'type', but I was old enough to know men who wear funky hats are to be avoided and it is *possible* he wore a fedora, which I had always believed was the international sign for letting people know you leave comments underneath online porn videos. But, in spite of his offensive hat, he had a confidence that was undeniable – although, in hindsight, I realise that he was just American, and you shouldn't be charmed by an American's confidence because they were born with it and it hasn't been earned.

His confidence was perhaps heightened by the fact that, during this particular leg of the trip, my friend Esther and I had amassed a group of very unconfident friends, due to my secret talent, which is that I possess some sort of Disney princess charm that draws meek and unconfident girls into my orbit.

There was one girl in particular, called Jessica, who was Irish and very much needed coaxing out of her shell. Esther and I would try to get her involved by buying rounds of shots and insisting she do them with us, at one point both of us chanting, 'Say Yessica!' over and over again until she did it. She spent a week with us, shyly accepting offers to go on walks or to beach parties, and we got to know Jessica quite well. By the end of the week, we started to see signs that she was feeling more confident; for example, during one of the hostel parties, she wore round glow-in-the-dark glasses and only once asked us if she was 'pulling it off'.

When it was time for her to leave the hostel, we gave her a heartfelt goodbye in the foyer before turning on our heels and returning to our group of friends, including David, who were playing a game of cards.

During the course of the card game, someone brought up the fact that Katie had left – in fact, we kept hearing the name Katie until eventually Esther asked who that was.

One of the Irish guys piped up, 'Katie! The girl you've been calling Jessica for the past week.'

I laughed as though he'd told a joke.

'I'm serious,' he said. 'The poor girl's name was Katie and you two thought it was Jessica. She told me she was too scared to say anything, so she just kept letting you call her that.'

I realised in that moment that, while I definitely lack confidence in many areas of my life, I don't think I'll ever understand what it feels like to have so little confidence that I let people call me the wrong name for a week.

After Katie had left, we began hanging out with David and his hat more and more, and he tried to kiss me every night. My initial repulsion to his advances only seemed to spur him on and, after weeks of relentless courting, I gave in. And in a tale as old as time, he retreated from me almost immediately, which meant I was now hooked.

While overseas, I had pursued a variety of men, all of whom seemed exotic, like they were portals into a different life I could never have imagined possible. These days, their names are portals into a late-night scroll on Facebook and the main cause of my permanently furrowed brow, thanks to the hours I have wasted trying to figure out whether we had sex near the Louvre or if they're my cousin's friend who once showed me his webbed toe.

But David felt different to me and, even though his interest in me had waned, I thought about him often and we kept in touch for the rest of my trip. Every now and then during one of our late-night text-message exchanges, I could goad him into admitting that he missed me, and when I returned to Australia, he totally encouraged me – although now I think about it, at most he may have simply agreed to my offer – to visit him in San Francisco.

I saved for months and flew to Los Angeles, where I was to board the cheap connecting flight to San Francisco I had purchased without reading even a single word of the fine print. Tired, hungover and manic, I approached the counter where a woman with smooth skin and clear eyes told me that, actually, I had purchased no baggage allowance and it would cost me two hundred dollars if I wanted to check in a suitcase for a domestic flight. She was not won over by my argument that my bag was only twelve kilos, and she explained that because the bag had a hard bottom it was considered luggage and not carry-on.

Feeling either sorry for me or benevolent, she leaned in and said, 'Listen, there's a bunch of big plastic sacks that were left here after some airport deliveries. You could put all your stuff into one of those and just ditch your suitcase.'

Spurred on by our perceived camaraderie, I laughed. 'I can't put all my things into a see-through sack. That's mental!'

'Okay, well, that will be two hundred dollars,' she replied, clearly over this exchange.

So everything went into the plastic sack and I skulked off to my gate. I tried a few different ways of holding the sack in the hopes that one position would look dignified, but in the end I just went with the classic over-the-shoulder, as though it was a new type of trendy bindle. I knew, deep down, that turning up with a sack would seem like the annoying tactic of a girl trying to secure her place as the 'protagonist' in whatever the fuck this reunion was. But careening towards David's apartment in a taxi I could barely afford, I still held out hope he might find it endearing.

I arrived at his apartment with my sexiest expression and the giant plastic sack of my belongings and, within a microsecond, I knew I'd made a huge mistake. He didn't mention the sack or even attempt a fake laugh in response to my pre-prepared quip about it. Instead, he welcomed me into his apartment, looking as though I'd interrupted his video game during a crucial moment, which I had.

For an entire week I stayed in his home, acutely aware that he didn't want me there. To this day, I believe that this is one of the worst feelings in the world. For most people – and this is definitely the case for me – we tend to reflect the way we're being treated in the moment. If someone is laughing at you, you start making more jokes; if they smile at you, you smile back. So when someone treats you like you're being annoying, you tend to lose your confidence and start being even *more* annoying. You can feel yourself doing and saying things that are just making it worse; it's almost as if their feelings towards you become contagious and you start becoming as annoyed at yourself as they are at you.

He'd half-heartedly wave goodbye to me in the morning and go to work, after which I'd explore the city, pretending to have fun. Ashamed that I'd created this entire love story in my mind and too embarrassed to admit to any of my friends what had happened, I would walk the streets of San Francisco alone, willing something to happen to me, even walking into the more dangerous parts of town – but, alas, even the local thieves could sense I wanted it too badly. David had got in my head so much that I even believed I was not worthy to be held at knifepoint.

On the second-last day, outside a Starbucks, I met a young Indian guy from Kerala, who told me he was training to be a pilot. After talking for a while, he invited me to have lunch at his place. This was because, being a white woman, I had mentioned my recent trip to India and discussed my favourite dish with him in the first five minutes of conversation. I went along with him, thinking that anything would be better than nothing. He was very nice and made me palak paneer as promised. We ate the curry and drank beers on his rooftop and, with the sun dappling my eye and a buzz from the alcohol, I could almost convince myself I was having a good time.

At some point between our third and fourth beer, he tried to kiss me. I said no, out of some strange loyalty to my reverse captor.

I'll always remember his sad eyes as he pleaded with me to stay. 'No, Becky, please, we have so much to talk about,' he said, as I tried to ignore his quite obvious erection.

I made some excuses about being late to meet a friend and bustled down the fire escape, stopping every few seconds to do a sort of semi-bow and thank him for the meal.

The next night, I walked around for as long as I could. In what was obviously a conscious effort to avoid me, David had taken to staying later and later at work, and I wanted to prove to him that it didn't bother me.

I looked up some potential things I could do and saw that George Clinton and the Parliament-Funkadelic were playing a small gig on the outskirts of town. I walked through the club door, which was just a thick layer of multicoloured streamers, and emerged on the other side to see ten or so beautiful women onstage in their underwear. It turned out it wasn't just a funk gig but also a 'Big Booty' competition, and the whole band was there to judge who had the best ass. The vibe was really fun and, despite the pangs of loneliness I felt looking around at big groups of friends laughing, I bought a beer and decided to enjoy myself.

Eventually a guy next to me offered me some of his joint and, thinking this was a sign that he was up for a chat, I got up onto my tiptoes.

'This is so cool,' I said into his ear.

'What?' he replied, moving his head away from my mouth, visibly irritated.

I projected more this time. 'This! This show is so cool.'

'Yeah ... Hey, we don't have to talk because I gave you weed, just so you know. I was being polite,' he replied, delivering the blow that almost extinguished all of my remaining self-esteem.

The frustrating thing was that he was quite unattractive and wearing a really pretentious flat cap. It was starting to feel like I was addicted to getting rejected by average men in bad hats.

I finished my beer and headed back into town, walking aimlessly with cold, aching feet. I eventually found myself googling 'entertainment San Francisco nearby' and Google suggested a famous comedy club called The Purple Onion. I had time to catch the late show, so I jumped in a cab and got there just in time to buy a ticket and another beer. I sat down and there, in the dark, alone, away from any man or hat, I finally felt that this might be ... something.

David, after having my self-esteem crushed and beaten down all week by your unwavering indifference, the idea of getting onstage and trying comedy suddenly didn't seem so scary. Eight years after this disastrous visit, I would return to America to do a set on Conan O'Brien's show and that's got to be partly thanks to you.

ATTN: HATERS

It might seem strange that this book, which is written by a woman and will be, I imagine, marketed to independent and modern women (the kind who have a copy of a Sally Rooney book on their bedside table, next to a Glasshouse candle and a bottle of melatonin) using the various media streams that target that demographic, would begin by thanking a man. But the truth is, there are a lot of men out there for whom I have a lot to thank, especially if this book is about thanking the ones I never thought I would.

To be clear, like anyone (or more specifically any woman), I can find myself loving and hating men in equal measure. But the idea of amassing a fanbase based purely on detesting them doesn't sit well with me. I'm sure the men who bought this book in an outward act of male allyship might be crestfallen (or elated!) to hear this.

That's not to say I'm not a feminist – of course I am. But then what does that actually mean? I am, by all means, living the feminist lifestyle that was marketed to me in my late teens and twenties, in that I make my own money and for the most part I don't rely on men, except when I need to torrent a movie or be driven somewhere (due to the fact I don't have my driver's licence). I suppose some people would even argue that by, at times, using a man's time and labour without paying for it, I have achieved true empowerment by enslaving those who ostensibly hold primary power.

What has always seemed odd to me is that feminism so often seems to march in step with the companies that make money off us, leaving us, or at least me, feeling alone and miserable.

I'm reminded of this when I find myself running at full speed on the treadmill, listening to a song by a perfect-looking nineteen-year-old girl telling me I don't need a man and I can do it alone. For a few brief, euphoric minutes, the endorphins from exercising flooding my brain, I believe that it's true, that I am all I need.

Then I take a shower, try to make eye contact with one of the blonde marketing zombies from my class, give up, and scroll my phone, only to come face to face with an IVF ad that's confused as to why I don't have a partner who is willing to have a baby with me. Companies use feminism to promote a sense of carefree nihilism, where you're encouraged to spend money on yourself and make selfish decisions, because us girls deserve it, right? So there I was in my twenties, with my girlboss cash buying serums and face masks, happily entering all my personal details into the Sephora website. But now I'm in my thirties and the Instagram ads targeted to me have a more solemn tone. They're now saying, 'Hmm, time to stop all that silliness and think about your future, babe. You can't party forever. Have you not met a man? What on earth have you been doing?' The same companies who used the broad strokes of feminism to encourage me to forget about the future and just buy the fifty-dollar lipstick are now happily selling my data on to other companies who are using it to imply I might be barren. And if not now, then soon.

But I don't mean to sound too depressing. My point is really that I am tired of feeling pressured to adhere to each generation's interpretation of feminism. In my opinion, the only way I can say something relevant in this book is by making sure it's how I actually feel, and I hope that this book endures despite a fluctuating cultural landscape. I don't see the point in my entire output as a woman being spent discussing only my grievances with men – I've succumbed to that type of discourse before and, looking back, I find it embarrassing that I, alone, on Twitter (a company owned by billionaire Jack Dorsey, who exclusively dates models), somehow managed to fail the Bechdel test.

By acknowledging that it's odd to kick off the book by thanking a man, I hope it expresses to you how important it is to me to find agency in the decisions I've made, and one way I've done that is by thanking men for their contributions, good and bad – an act that, to me, has felt most empowering of all.

The Chuckle Hut Comedy and Magic Club

I started working at the Chuckle Hut Comedy and Magic Club as a bartender in my early twenties. The place was operating at a loss and would shut its doors a few years later, something the owner, Mitch, seemed to already foresee during my employment. Mitch spent most of his time sitting in his office and staring at the wall while repetitively raking one of those mini meditative sandboxes. He had bought the place with his maladjusted brother John, who, before I worked there, had disappeared without a trace for a couple of months and then re-emerged one night, claiming he'd knocked his head badly on some rocks down at Sandgate and had suffered from a long bout of amnesia. It wasn't long before one of his friends outed him –

he'd apparently been crashing at a mate's place, smoking bongs and avoiding child-support payments.

Anyway, John was around a lot and, when he wasn't blind drunk, his brother would let him get up and do some comedy as a way of distracting him from poking his red drinker's nose into the finances.

The Chuckle Hut Comedy and Magic Club was sort of a scam – or, at least, it employed a business model based on the premise that there were enough people in the city that they could rip off everyone at least once. The only return customers they ever had was when people came back to retrieve a jacket they'd left on a chair.

The way they'd get customers in was by sending out official-looking letters to people in the suburbs, telling them they'd won four free tickets to a magic and comedy show for their birthday. Once everyone arrived on the night, the staff would herd all 500 of them into a large room with a makeshift stage. (During the week, this room was used for business conferences and other functions, as a way of making extra cash, so one of our main jobs at the start of a weekend shift was dragging in all the tables and chairs from storage as well as assembling said stage for the performers.) The staff then had the difficult task of explaining to the unsuspecting victims that, in order to redeem their free tickets, they had to buy dinner and at least one drink. Surprisingly, people nearly always did. They mostly came ready to party – the women would order white wines with lemonade, ice cubes and a dash of lime cordial, and the men would order jugs of rum and coke, plus dessert at the end and a hot mocha to wake them up before the drive home. I was regularly given the job of having to clean up diarrhoea in the toilets or, on some of our crazier nights, in the carpark, up against the wall.

There were always a few comedians on, but the headliner, at least while I worked there, was a bleach-blond hypnotist magician called Pauly B, who wore a rhinestone-studded leather jacket and a bright white smile, and drove a zippy little car with his face on it.

Pauly B would warm up the crowd with ten minutes of short clips from *Australia's Funniest Home Videos* and a few standard joke-book jokes. Then he would ask the crowd for a couple of volunteers to come onstage and undergo his special brand of hypnosis. Men in pale-blue jeans and sports jackets would race to be the first with their hand in the air, proving already that they were show-offs. He'd purposefully pick the ones who had the most people cheering for them, because it meant more pressure for them to go along with it.

Most of the time they were blue-collar workers around the age of fifty, who, by that stage of the show, were ten drinks deep and essentially already hypnotised. He'd seat them all next to each other and heavily imply that they were all gay, which would get huge laughs from the crowd. The lights would go down, a vaguely Middle Eastern tune would ring out over the hall, and a hush would fall over the glassy-eyed crowd as Pauly B began to perform hypnosis on the volunteers. Then *bang!* He'd put them under and make them act like chickens. People would roar with laughter watching their boss or father-in-law peck at the ground and squawk – though, if you looked closely at the men onstage, you could see the corners of their mouths slightly turned up into a smile, as they clearly enjoyed the attention. Then, out of nowhere, a recording of a ringing phone would start and he would tell them to answer it and say hello one by one.

Ring, ring.

'Hello?' one would say.

'Hi there,' Pauly B would reply in a terrible Indian accent, 'I'm a telemarketer calling to see if you wanted to upgrade your phone plan.' He'd smirk at the crowd at this point, then break character and ask the man, 'Now, what do you want to say to this telemarketer?'

'Fuck off, you curry muncher!' the hypnotised dunce would scream.

And the crowd would go crazy!

Pandering to a drunk suburban crowd was what Pauly B did best. Plus, as an added bonus, he'd cleverly devised a way to get around having to be the one who said anything racist by just getting the volunteers to do it. Not that he needed to worry about causing offence – to my knowledge, not a single audience member ever complained about that joke.

One customer was a big fan of Pauly B, and would regularly come to his shows, where he would hit on the younger female audience members and bar staff. There were rumours that this customer was a former paedophile – a phrase I always found odd, as I didn't realise you could be a *former* paedophile. I thought it was pretty much one of those things that, once was, always will be. For what it's worth, I don't think he was a paedophile. I think it's just something you call someone when they're kind of creepy and you don't like them. He did go home with a much younger female waitress one night, but if a man in his early forties who sleeps with girls in their twenties is considered a paedophile, then every male comedian I know is one. Sometimes I forget that I'm in my thirties now, and no man who is making a pass at me can ever be considered a paedophile, no matter how much older than me he is. The truth is I'm now at an age where I'm too old for an older man to even consider me a 'younger woman'. The mind boggles.

Like this customer, Pauly B also had a penchant for much younger women, and once slept with a female bartender. It always made me laugh that she went to his house to have a one-night stand with him, even though he lived an hour away from the club. It's actually quite admirable to commit to going home with a sober man with a solid hour's drive ahead of you. What on Earth do you talk about? I asked the bartender what they had discussed on the trip.

She shrugged. 'We didn't really talk much at all,' she said.

'He had a Tony Robbins self-help tape playing and we just sort of listened to that for the whole drive.'

When I asked her about his house, she told me he lived in this weird soulless mansion on one of the canals at the Gold Coast. It had once belonged to his late aunty, who had been jailed for defrauding a large number of people out of their retirement money. This didn't surprise me – fraudster is one of the three main vocations you can choose when you live on the Gold Coast, the other two being tattoo artist and owner of a dog-fighting ring.

She said the house had barely any furniture in it, but she did confirm that he had a large plush bed with black satin sheets, which was something I had always taken bets on with people at work. Apparently once they got to his house, he made her wait in the sparse lounge room while he cleansed, toned and moisturised. After twenty minutes of waiting around, he then called her into the bedroom as he was finishing up a round of push-ups, to make his muscles pop.

I asked her if he talked about magic at all. She said he refused to discuss anything magic-related with her and asked her not to bring up the subject.

Every night at the comedy club, the show would drag on, each punchline the same as the night before. If I was lucky, a fight might break out between tables and provide some relief to the monotony. Sometimes my comedian friends would do a warmup spot before the magic show, and they'd stick around after to keep me company. But on nights when it was just me behind the bar, I would grow restless as the faces that approached me got more and more raggedy.

I once found myself consoling a girl in the bathroom who was crying about how ugly she felt. On a whim, and in a bid to connect with her, I decided to reveal to her my own insecurities. Half an hour later, I had to kick her out of the venue for being enthusiastically fingered by her boyfriend near one of the speakers. I can only assume she was feeling more confident after our chat.

If I was desperate enough, I'd talk to the manager, Derek. He used to stand by the enclosed bar, blocking any potential escape, and perform his own little comedy routines while the comedians were onstage. I'd do my own little routine by pretending I didn't understand him.

'Check out that chick.' He'd point at a blonde in a bandeau dress. 'She makes me want to pitch a tent,' he'd say, both eyebrows raised.

'What do you mean?' I'd reply innocently.

'That girl … she, with my … never mind,' and he'd toddle off and try it again with someone else.

After three long hours, the show would end. Once everyone had left, the lights would turn back on and we'd pack away the plastic chairs and watch the magician gather his things. It's incredible what turning on a bright light can do to kill a magician's allure – I think the opposite of magic has got to be a man packing his props into a plastic crate under fluorescent lighting. I used to love watching him, his formerly animated face now all droopy and stern, holding a plastic chicken while actively ignoring the idiotic ramblings of Derek, who was desperate to make someone laugh by the end of the night.

I was actually invited to Derek's fiftieth birthday party, after only two weeks of working there. The last thing I remember was politely smiling and agreeing with something he'd said and, before I knew it, I had agreed to be picked up at 5 am from my home in a '96 Honda Civic to go on an all-day chartered fishing trip with him and five other men from work.

The next morning, Derek picked me up at 5 am as planned. Also in the car was one of the chefs, Cole – who used to pick meat out of people's pasta with his fingers if they requested a vegetarian meal – and my only ally at the comedy club, Dan, a cerebral redhead who, like me, lacked the constitution for declining birthday invitations and, as it would turn out, the open sea.

Dan and I were both starting out in comedy, and we sheepishly admitted to each other before the car ride that we had only accepted the invitation in the hope that we might form relationships with some of the core staff, who might then book us to do one of the comedian spots at the club. We were always looking for stage time.

Once we were all in the car, Derek passed around a bunch of joints with his fat sausage fingers. By the time we got to the pier, I had lost my grip on reality and, considering my actual reality, wasn't even sure I wanted it back.

After fussing about for ages, we set out for sea – just me, Dan, Derek, Cole and three bearded men. The combination of the rolling sea and the old man's weed had Dan and me back to back in the foetal position within half an hour. Even though we were similarly afflicted, we were both so sick and stoned that we couldn't communicate anything to each other, so it was pretty much the same as being alone.

At one point, the same fat sausage fingers that had passed me the joint in the car started feeding me salami and cheese sandwiches cut into squares. As I was quite hungry, I begrudgingly accepted them, but threw up about ten minutes later.

As I gripped the silver rail, recovering from my last heave, Cole handed me a hook and a small baitfish and told me I had better throw in a line or I'd waste the whole day. I took the fish and tried to secure it onto the hook, but it kept slipping off. After a few tries, it had so many punctures in it that it was unusable. I was still so stoned I wasn't sure if this was funny or if I was in trouble. I looked over at Dan, who I thought might be able to help with the fish, but I could see that *he* was now being fed the salami and cheese sandwiches. I told Cole I needed to lie back down.

When I woke up, we were back at the dock and all the men were holding up large fish, except Dan, who was vomiting over the other side of the boat.

On the drive home, Dan and I were both exhausted and feeble, but also very aware of what a good story this would be to tell our friends. When Derek stopped for petrol and the others got out to stretch their legs, Dan lamented to me that he couldn't even afford this trip and was freaking out about his finances. Looking down at the vomit caked on his shirt, I didn't have the heart to tell him that I hadn't been asked to pay.

Thank you to the Chuckle Hut Comedy and Magic Club, not only for the opportunity to meet so many people starting out in comedy, some of whom remain my closest friends today, but also for the reminder that nearly all magicians are weird.

Carlos

The first time I laid eyes on Carlos, he was licking a bit of carpet, high on mushrooms. Carlos was the sort of guy you might catch stealing twenty dollars out of your purse and have no qualms about forgiving immediately. He was so effortlessly charming that he made whomever he was with feel like they'd arrived just in time to save him from boredom. Even when you saw him make someone else feel this way, you didn't take it personally; it was like you shared a secret with him, like he was only performing for everyone else and not you.

I met Carlos one year at the Woodford Folk Festival, which, if you're over forty, is a week-long celebration of culture and music, but if you're twenty, like we were at the time, it is just a party. My cousin and his friends would go to the festival every year, and this year I'd decided to join them. I had actually been a few times with my mum, because she had performed there as a musician, but, up until this particular year, my time there had been fairly subdued. I'd been drunk and stoned, sure, but always with the looming deadline of having to return to the tent I shared with my mum and pretend to be sober. The trick, by the way, to appearing sober in front of a parent is to be the same petulant self you are when you're not drunk or high. For some reason, teenagers trying to cover up the fact that they're drunk or high seem to think that the best plan of attack is to be extra chatty, engaging and bright with their parents, which, for my mum, would immediately arouse suspicion.

This particular year, though, I camped with my cousin at his friends' campsite, which had been set up by one of those men who know how things go together and who at some point in their lives will drive around Australia in their customised truck. He had brought carpet and couches and set up beams of wood that connected together perfectly to form a semi-permanent structure that was so comfortable, barely anyone left the campsite to actually enjoy the festival.

I went into the grounds a couple of times, but regularly found myself annoyed at the groups of hippies who roamed in big packs, sometimes while on stilts or hula-hooping completely naked, and who would stare at me accusatorially as I tried to move past them. The thing about hippies is that they're just regular people who have the same selfish desires as the rest of us, but never engage in an actual discussion long enough to be called out on it. It's all peace, love and sharing until they're cutting in front of you in the line for food – and if you say anything, you need to 'relax'.

It wasn't just the hippies. The whole thing was a bit of a pain in the neck, to be honest. I'd have to queue to get inside the festival, queue to get something to eat, and figure out which artist I wanted to watch. And after all that, I'd constantly find myself at the wrong tent. There I'd be, holding a plate of overpriced lentil curry, trying to decide whose armpit was the least gross to be under, and having to watch an hour and a half of a women's choir or, worse, a slam poetry semi-final. The thing about slam poetry is that it's not very good. It seems like anything can be slam poetry if people just talkreallyfast and then SLOOOOW it right down. I don't even know how I feel about poetry in general; I think I'm too impatient for it. The only kind I've ever enjoyed is when a friend is drunk-texting me and keeps accidentally hitting the return key.

Where are you
I need
Help
Might get kebab first
Then come

I have always thought music festivals were so hot and awful, and I could never understand the endless amounts of energy people had around me. My heart would sink every time someone suggested another tent, another band, another bar. After six drinks (which included hours of lining up for said drinks, then needing to piss almost immediately), my entire body would be aching with fatigue and all I'd want to do was get something fried I could eat off a stick and find somewhere to lie down.

So back to the campsite I would go.

I at least vaguely knew the thirty or so people staying at the campsite, but Carlos was new. He seemed immediately popular, which made the light he shone on me every now and then feel like even more of a blessing.

On the first day, Carlos made mushroom brownies and invited neighbouring camps over to party with us. He was great at introductions and knew just who would get along best.

On the second day, one of his new friends brought around some 'really good acid', and I watched on as everyone let this man in a corset drop it into their water bottles. Carlos asked me if I wanted to try it and I flat-out rejected the idea – it seemed like one of the drugs on the 'too far' list, one that would make you mental.

It didn't take long, however, for persuasive Carlos to convince me to try the acid. I was terrified of what would happen, certain I would die. Instead, about half an hour later, I was overcome with the most intense euphoria, the kind I hadn't experienced since being a child, which is to say I was just living in the moment, which is where all the good feelings are apparently.

I don't want to go on some Kerouacian rant about how I felt, but let's just say that day I finally understood the appeal of music festivals. Every conversation I had was the most interesting; every idea I had was a genius one (and everyone around me seemed to agree); every mud puddle was worth looking at, sitting in, playing with. I couldn't care less about what anyone thought of me then or in the future. And the whole campsite was feeling the same way.

That is one thing about getting older that makes me sad. When you're younger, you share such close, chemically induced moments with people you barely know, and there's next to no possibility of that happening to me now. In my day-to-day life, there's a very slim chance I'll end up in peals of laughter with a girl wearing fairy wings. Those people probably don't even exist anymore. It's not that the girl with fairy wings is dead, but she probably lives in Geelong with two kids and a husband who's a cop.

It's funny, because, now I've done most drugs, I find it hard to empathise with someone who's scared of them. In those moments, I should remember that I am now Carlos and the scared person is me before my first acid trip.

There was a time once, not too long ago, when I found myself hanging out with a famous Australian comedian in his late forties. I asked him if he'd like to join me and another comedian as we smoked a joint. He told me that he has never touched the stuff, and that he knew a guy from his hometown who had smoked weed and then killed himself.

I didn't say it, but I remember thinking that the guy was probably going to kill himself anyway. The weed he was smoking had probably been one of the few things that helped him get through the day.

What was funny was that the forty-something-year-old comedian kept insisting that he *would* try it, definitely, at some point, 'but not tonight because I have an early flight in the morning'. He then proceeded to drink fourteen vodka sodas and pass out while slumped against the wall standing up.

It reminded me of that time at Woodford Folk Festival, where I'd first done acid, when a brother of my friend's friend turned up to the campsite with a carton of Jack Daniels and his own camping chair, and just sat and watched us all in turns melting towards each other and then rolling away, while continually commenting that we were 'random'. If someone said something outrageous, he'd exclaim that it was 'awkward', which it wasn't — at least not for us.

Later in the night, at the back of an outdoor amphitheatre in the festival, I watched the trees breathing in and out, and discovered a newfound willingness to forgive anyone who had ever caused me pain. As I was taking in all the tiny acts of humanity happening around me, my friend's friend's brother's face popped up into view and he breathed, 'I'm so fucking wasted.' The hot stench of bourbon stung my eyes. It felt like an ungodly act.

The morning after, I opened my eyes and stared at the tent's ceiling while listening to Carlos have a spirited conversation with someone about the ethics of euthanasia. From the smell of bacon and eggs, I could tell things were back to normal, at least until the afternoon.

We passed the week like this, all of us dancing, laughing, repeating our inside jokes, until one morning towards the end of the festival, Carlos had disappeared. It was a morning like all the others, until someone noticed his tent had been packed up so neatly, there wasn't a trace that he'd ever been there. Well, there was probably some of his DNA on one of the couches – he had seduced at least four of the girls we were camping with, including one who had a boyfriend who was not a fan of Carlos.

As people slowly came out of their tents, the others would ask them if they knew where Carlos was or why he'd left. But no one did.

Some people were upset that Carlos had left without a goodbye, but I stood by him for the way he left. Sometimes the nicest thing you can do is leave without saying goodbye, particularly in a party setting. Some people are obsessed with doing the goodbyes and, frankly, it's no good for anyone. Why even remind other people who are still invested in the party that leaving is an option? You'll be at the pinnacle of a good story when someone comes over to explain why they have to leave: 'Well, I'm off, guys, I've got tennis in the morning.' Yes, we know, we heard your little song and dance to three other groups of people before you reached us.

Eventually, the conversation at the campsite turned to who might know where he'd gone, and that turned into a discussion of who knew him best, and after some time it became apparent that no one had known Carlos at all. It turned out that every person at the campsite had only met him at the start of the week and assumed he was a friend of someone else.

I still think it's one of the funniest things anyone has ever done. He must have just been walking by on the first day, seen the incredible set-up, and realised that the campsite had everything it needed except him.

In recent years, the thought of trying to contact Carlos online has occasionally crossed my mind. But what would be the point? We'd had a good time, and now I don't ever have to see him in a suit or read the questionable things he might share on Facebook. He'll remain forever alive in my mind the way he wanted to be seen.

So thank you to Carlos for teaching me that sometimes not saying goodbye is the perfect way to leave.

My primary school girl group

I was walking with my friend the other day when we saw a group of noisy miner birds pecking one of their own to death. We were both horrified but kept walking – obviously, we couldn't intervene, and everyone knows birds regularly turn on each other.

I would have thought that having humans as a common enemy meant animals of the same species would have some kind of loyalty towards each other, like, 'Hey, I know we aren't always gonna get along, but I'm a bird and you're a bird, so let's look out for each other, okay?' But rarely does that seem to happen.

Then I thought about it for just one second more and realised that you could make the exact same argument for human beings, and look at what we're capable of doing to each other. And I'm not even talking about the worst examples – the ruthlessness of human nature can be witnessed in the schoolyard, particularly among the large groups of schoolgirls who congregate together each lunchtime.

We might not have pecked each other to death, but the girl group I was in at primary school definitely had a strict pecking order. We were kept in line using cruel tactics, such as choosing new locations to sit at lunchtime and 'forgetting' to tell one or two girls. The journey to becoming accepted into what was widely known by all to be the more popular group was long and arduous. It consisted of trying to inch your way into the centre of the circle, where the coolest girl would be holding court, doing something like playing with a flower, already secure in the knowledge of how beautiful she was.

In order to get to the middle of the circle, you'd begin your social campaign by starting in on some of the weaker girls on the outside. These were the ones who were barely clinging on to their position themselves, so they would be happy to talk to you in order to at least look busy and somewhat popular themselves. If you played your cards right and managed to entertain them, it was possible that a girl closer to the middle would be intrigued by what you had to say and start up a conversation, allowing you to then inch in a little closer, pushing someone else out to the edge.

Eventually, after many lunchtimes of inching, you would miraculously find yourself quite close to the popular girl, and if, like me, you could braid hair to a proficient level, you would be allowed to braid hers. This proximity would give you some time to shine and prove your worth in the centre, which, if done successfully, could really solidify your position in the group.

It was important to keep your eye on the prize and remember that it was every girl for themselves. Having worked my way to the middle, I'd sometimes look up and accidentally make eye contact with some of my former outer-edge comrades who had taken a shot on me. They'd give me an imploring look, and I could see they wanted me to return the favour and help them climb the ranks too. But I'd shrug apologetically and try to telepathically communicate that there was nothing I could do right now.

The concept of a group sleepover always seemed like a fun idea, but most of them turned into a Russian Roulette–like game of 'Who is going to cry first?' There were plenty of activities designed to fracture friendships and destroy alliances and, because of that, there was always a chance you might emerge triumphant.

I found that most of the tension at a sleepover came from the girls constantly vying for a higher position or to at least have their current position reaffirmed to them. Then you had the girls who knew they had power and that there would always be someone who wanted to take it away.

You never knew how a sleepover was going to go down. I once saw a girl go from outer edge to inner circle simply by staying up the latest. The stakes were high, and you had to be brave enough to risk it all, knowing it could go either way. Do you dare put shaving cream on the popular girl's face while she's asleep, knowing she might either find the prank hysterical or banish you to the outer edges forever? What about accusing a girl of stealing something from your bag to get her on the back foot? These were both tactics I saw employed at some point to varying degrees of success.

If somebody suggested a game of 'Spice Girls', it was not merely a game, it was a way for the group to discover how much power each one had. It always seemed to me that the boys would play games like football, cricket or marbles, which had set rules and the fun was had in playing the game to the best of your ability. But for us girls, the fun lay in deciding the intricate rules and the framework for how the game was going to be played.

'You want to be Posh? No, Jess is Posh now. You can be Sporty Spice.' And with that, you'd basically been labelled sexless.

Of course, the popular girl with blonde hair would always get to be Baby Spice. My Czechoslovakian friend, Adrianna, on the other hand, who had blonde hair but no status, was delegated to Scary Spice every time because she was considered the most exotic of us all. The conversation over who was who, and why such-and-such deserved to be a particular Spice Girl, was so long and fraught that by the time all the particulars had been nutted out, no one actually wanted to play anymore and everyone had had their feelings hurt.

There was one sleepover I went to in Year Seven, where a particularly sadistic girl in the group suggested a game. First, we would all sit on the bed and put our names into a hat. Then we'd draw out one name, and that girl would have to stand alone in front of the bed while all the girls on the bed took turns saying what they found annoying about her – and the girl being critiqued was not allowed to get upset. The idea of the game, this girl explained, was to learn to accept that we all have flaws and to help each other address these flaws in a mature and helpful way.

'Plus we'll all have our time being told what's wrong with us, so it's fair,' she added.

The first girl lasted thirty seconds before bursting into tears and running out of the room. She then locked herself in the bathroom for the rest of the night, at one point threatening to eat some aspirin she'd found in the top drawer. This meant the sleepover became mostly dedicated to dealing with this drama, as different girls took turns trying to convince her to come out and just have a good time. Meanwhile, the instigator of the game sat there, delighted at what she'd achieved.

This game was undoubtedly cruel, but I was secretly disappointed that it didn't go on a bit longer. Deep down, I had this strange desire to hear what everyone disliked about me. Perhaps the most frustrating thing about a group of women is that they won't tell you exactly what it is you're doing wrong; instead, it's up to you to pick up on subtle hints and clues. I was jealous of the ease of male friendships – among the boys, any bad behaviour was up for public discussion and ridicule, so you at least had the chance to defend yourself.

Of course, most of these sorts of mind games fade away by the time you're older and have found your real female friends. I now have so many beautiful friends who I adore and feel completely comfortable around, and who make me feel loved in a way I didn't think I ever would be. I sometimes look around at them and think I've found the best women in the world.

That being said, I don't think any girl groups, no matter what age their members are, are immune to the politics of female friendship. I also have some female friends who, once we're in a group together, make me feel like I'm getting sucked back into the dynamic of that primary school circle. There's a bitchiness in groups of women that I'm addicted to and terrified of. I think it's one of the great allures of women in general – that no matter how hard you try, you can't ever truly know what they're thinking or who they're colluding with. And once you realise that, you can be truly free of the circle.

So thank you to my primary school girl group for the vital lesson that still applies today: you only need a handful of completely trustworthy female friends and the rest are just there to have fun and figure out the rules of the game with.

The Westfield shopping centre

In my early twenties, I worked at the customer service desk of a Westfield shopping centre in north Brisbane. My friend Sophie had got me the job, which I was to start over the Christmas break, and I was excited to begin as I had always been a huge fan of going to the shops. It's seen by my friends and loved ones as one of my little provincial quirks, like my love for theme parks. To me, theme parks are a great equaliser – the man next to me on the ride might have a neck tattoo and a dubious relationship with his ex-wife, but, for now, we're both sitting side by side squealing in terror and delight.

If you grew up in a suburb forty minutes out of the city, like I did for most of my young life, you may understand why a

Westfield shopping centre has such a special place in my heart. I have a theory that any place that's forty minutes out of the city is the worst. People who live there will commute to the city for everything they need, which means the suburb itself gets neglected. The people who live an hour out of the city, however, have decided that they aren't going all that way on a regular basis for the things they like, so they'd better hunker down and make their suburb or town somewhere decent.

For me, a trip to the Westfield shopping centre meant that Mum and I were on a mission together. It represented a certain type of calmness from having enough money to treat ourselves. In my eyes, it was a gateway to the world, a cosmopolitan retreat from our suburb, filled with all the brands from TV, and the possibility of McDonald's for dinner.

The customer service desk I worked at was in the middle of the shopping centre, directly underneath a beam of natural light that perfectly illuminated us customer service reps and made it easier for irate customers to locate us. My first day working there, a woman in a maxi dress with two children in tow came barrelling towards the desk.

'Do you know that in the level three toilets there's a poo on top of the toilet seat?' she shrieked, as if I had been personally responsible for the deed.

'Um, no, I wasn't aware of that … particular one,' I responded, warily eyeing the large diamond ring that sat below one of her perfectly manicured nails.

'Well, it's *disgusting*,' she spat, which I couldn't disagree with.

'I've just spilled my mocha on the ground. What are *you* going to do about it?' yelled another woman behind her.

'I'm going to get on all fours and lick it up like a dog,' I considered replying.

But the main thing people were upset about was the new Westfield policy, which declared that if people had been at the shopping centre for longer than two hours, then they had to pay for their parking.

'It goes against our most basic human rights,' one man said aggressively, a glob of his spittle landing on my temple. It was bizarre how many times people's spittle would land on my face and the person who'd done it would see it happen and fail to apologise. It wasn't out of embarrassment, but out of what I presume was an assumption that I wouldn't complain or wasn't even really allowed to.

To combat this growing resentment around paid parking, and to boost customer morale, Westfield employees were occasionally given parking vouchers and ordered to hand them out to customers randomly. We were told to be careful doing this, that we weren't to create a mob-like atmosphere or let it get 'out of control', as there had been instances in other centres where people were injured by human stampedes during previous prize giveaways. Imagine being crushed to death by a human stampede – it's a death so undignified, I imagine your family would prefer to say you'd died during a wild night of autoerotic asphyxiation gone wrong.

Whenever I was sent out on one of these expeditions, I found that it always took a while to get going, because whenever you'd attempt to hand out the vouchers, people would assume you were trying to sell them something and they'd shoo you away or avoid eye contact. Then a more astute customer would pick up on what was being offered and, within seconds, you'd find yourself swamped by shoppers elbowing each other out of the way and demanding free parking vouchers. I remember giving out two passes, valued at about four dollars, to a man who was so overjoyed, he started breakdancing while holding a bag of Donut King donuts. I'm sure, outside of the shopping centre, these were all intelligent and caring people; it's just what that place does to you.

Over time, I realised that I had to leave my humanity at the door and succumb to the abuse. It was my own ego that made me continue to feel hurt by the customers; I was refusing to accept that we live in a world where people in service positions are treated like shit by those who think it's okay to do that, and, honestly, once I got over trying to be seen as an actual person, I was able to really enjoy myself.

One afternoon, I was trying to help a middle-aged woman with an expired gift voucher. I was highly aware of her speaking to me like she was being so generous and benevolent by engaging with me. She spoke in clipped tones, a barely concealed sneer dancing over her lips. Then her kid, who I had gone to school with, came up from behind her and started chatting with me. I really enjoyed watching her entire demeanour change as she realised our interaction was no longer anonymous.

Even though I loved going to Westfield as a kid and teenager, until I worked there, I didn't realise how many people went to the shopping centre every day and stayed there from open to close. There was an older husband-and-wife couple whom we all knew, who loved spending all day at the shops, eating ice creams and looking at things. The husband needed a mobility scooter to get around, but his wife could walk.

A couple of weeks after I started, the husband ran his scooter right over his wife's foot, breaking it in three places, which meant we didn't seem them for about six weeks. Then, on my last day, I saw the two of them ambling along. The woman's foot had healed and the man was once again atop his mobility scooter. I ran back to the customer service desk and told everyone they were back, and the news really lifted our spirits.

An hour later, my manager told me that the security guard had just radioed in to tell her that, while the couple had been perusing a popular homewares store, the husband had accidentally accelerated into a display of vases, freaked out, then reversed over his wife's foot, breaking it again.

My friend still works at that Westfield and he tells me that they're still together to this day, which I see as a testament not just to the strength of their relationship but to their love of going to the shops.

When visiting a Westfield, you may have occasionally noticed a bird fly through the front doors, and, if you look up, you'll see them flying around in circles in the highest part of the roof. You may have even seen them perched on one of the benches next to a tired old man who's having a sit-down while his wife tries on various capri pants in a nearby store.

I would sometimes see people pointing and laughing at the sight of a little bird lost inside a shopping centre. Admittedly, it is funny to see something in a place it shouldn't be, but a bird inside a shopping centre is much more tragic than they realised. You see, if a bird gets caught inside of a shopping centre, it usually only has an hour or so before it dies of exhaustion or thirst from the stress and general discombobulation of being inside a manmade environment.

I suppose it's similar to what might happen to a human trapped in a shopping centre, if there wasn't a huge food court for them to hydrate and feed themselves – certainly there were times when I saw people experiencing the same levels of confusion and distress. I used to have to help people find the exit of the shopping centre nearly every day. It's commonplace for people to either lose themselves or their toddlers at a Westfield; in fact, they're designed to increase the chances of that happening. Next time you're in a shopping centre, pause for a second and try to remember who you are and why you went there. It's almost impossible. You become convinced that you *need* bejewelled jeans and a Dyson vacuum, when really you only went in there to shit on the top of a toilet seat.

The Christmas I worked at Westfield was a regular Queensland summer, which meant it was too hot most of the time. Sometimes the air was so dense and humid that you wouldn't even notice yourself breathing. One benefit of working in a Westfield shopping centre was being able to spend all day in air conditioning, though it didn't save me from agitated customers who, having come straight from the blistering heat outside, would arrive red-faced at the customer service counter, already pissed off at the cut of my jib.

It wasn't just the heat that made people irate. In the days leading up to Christmas, when shops began to sell out of products, everywhere you'd look there were people in the grips of panic. It wasn't unusual to hear of grown men and women rolling around on the floor, clutching either side of a stuffed Peppa the Pig toy and insisting they had got to it first. Mums would be found bawling their eyes out in the aisles of Smiggle, while fourteen-year-old sales assistants kept repeating that they were sorry but that sparkly notebook sold out weeks ago.

The night before Christmas Eve, myself and a few of the other customer service girls were idling around behind the desk when a man in a hi-vis vest approached, holding about ten bags and a shopping list that, he told me, had been written by his wife. He was looking for a Buddha statue for the garden and all the places he had tried were sold out. He explained that it was the last item on the list and he couldn't go home until he'd found one. I told him that I empathised, but I wasn't really sure if I could help him. All I could do was point out a few places that might have one.

As I started reading out from the store directory, his face became red and tears sprang to his eyes. 'I just tried there! They don't have any left! I just need a fucking Buddha statue so I can get the fuck out of here!'

Then, as a full stop to what I felt was already a pretty strong outburst, he head-butted the counter, quite hard. He apologised immediately and ran off before I could properly react.

One of the girls leant over and said, 'Talk about toxic masculinity.'

I agreed, but all I could think in that moment was that I had never felt so sorry for anyone. It may have been a display of toxic masculinity, but toxic femininity was making your husband try to find a Buddha statue in a Westfield shopping centre two days before Christmas.

Thank you to Westfield, for the opportunity to experience what it's like behind the customer service desk and for teaching me that your 36-hour shopping period is to be avoided at all costs.

Jack

One afternoon, around 2016, I found myself moping around in a house I shared with some friends in Leichhardt, Sydney. It was during a period that I can only describe as the worst part of my twenties – somewhere between the ages of twenty-seven and twenty-nine, when I started to realise that my destructive behaviour was not as cute or interesting as it had once seemed. I was in the middle of processing the end of what was a very difficult relationship, and I use the term 'processing' loosely, as I still to this day don't know exactly what happened there. Even now, I don't want to write anything too detailed about that particular ex, as the thought of him frantically turning the pages of this book looking for signs of his impact on me and finding nothing (besides this) gives me a sense of satisfaction that therapists would probably describe as 'unhealthy'.

As I lay on the couch, occasionally breaking from staring into the middle distance to scoop some dip onto a chip, my roommate Gerard came tripping down the stairs and told me he was going to set me up with one of his friends. This particular friend, Jack, had just told him that he was sick to death of dating beautiful women and wanted to start going out with smart ones. Gerard thought I'd be perfect.

This was funny to hear, because now I knew for sure that Gerard did not think I was beautiful. At least he thought I was smart, I suppose, though I had never thought of myself as especially clever.

It didn't come as a complete shock that Gerard didn't consider me beautiful. I'm sort of used to it; for some reason, people have always felt very comfortable making comments about how I look, often in the same casual tone they'd use when commenting on the weather or a bright parrot they've just seen in a nearby tree. I was once sleeping with a guy who used to marvel at the fact that he could get hard with me, as I wasn't up to his usual standard – and he would say this brightly, as if he were giving me a compliment.

Because of this experience, I now find myself scared of being complimented, because so often a compliment is followed by an insult. This fear may also be a symptom of talking to people after my stand-up comedy shows. Every time a sentence begins with a compliment about my set, I can feel myself tensing up while I wait for them to get to the bit where they tell me what was wrong with it.

Take the woman who approached me after a set a few years ago. 'I just think you're so funny,' she said, then, before I could feel too pleased, she quickly added, 'but I hope my daughter doesn't end up like you.'

I think, from their perspective, it's because they've just seen me onstage having people clap and cheer for me – so, for the sake of my now-overinflated ego, it's up to them to bring me back down to earth and make sure I don't feel too good about myself.

The thing is, I don't! That's why I'm up onstage yearning to please a crowd of strangers in the first place.

I just seem to encounter these backhanded complimenters everywhere I go. I recently had a girl at a party approach me and tell me that she liked my hair. Before I had time to say 'thank you', she added, 'Because it used to be a bit too thick and puffy.'

I knew it was my own fault for not getting out of there quickly enough. I had foolishly let my guard down and paid the price.

Regardless, I chose to ignore the second part and still thanked her, then turned around in an attempt to find another friend to talk to. But it was too late. She went in for round two.

'Hey, you're my age, aren't you? About twenty-five?'

'No,' I replied cautiously. 'I'm thirty-one actually.'

And her face fell. 'Aww, that's okay,' she said placatingly.

And that's what can happen if you don't remain vigilant.

I never thought much about how I or other people looked until I was in my late twenties. In high school, my friends would discuss in detail who among us was the most beautiful and why, but I never had much to add to the conversation. To me, there didn't seem to be that much of a difference between us in terms of attractiveness; we were all young and glowing and fun to be around.

In order to make someone interested in you, I thought you had to be able to say something smart or cutting, but it turns out you just had to have certain features and measurements, like big boobs and a slightly upturned nose. I don't know why it took me so long to realise this, because I'm yet to come across a man who's gotten an erection from laughing at a good quip I made at their expense.

I first came to this realisation about men when I went travelling with one of my beautiful friends, and noticed that while I received polite smiles and was required to pay full price for all my drinks at bars, my friend had men following her up and down the street, tripping up the stairs and ripping their eyes out just to talk to her. Any of the male attention I thought I was receiving was actually ricocheting off her and onto me.

For this reason, I've always felt sort of left out when women talk about being harassed by strange, creepy men. I remember years ago, there was a viral video where a woman wearing jeans and a black crewneck T-shirt recorded all the catcalls and wolf-whistles she got when walking along the streets in New York City with a hidden camera. I knew I was supposed to share the video in indignant feminine rage, but a part of me was thinking, *Fuck, that never happens to me.* If I ever get catcalled or whistled at, I will probably just assume the man doing it needs help lifting something heavy out of a van.

It does seem exhausting being so gorgeous. There must be a weariness that comes from knowing that people are only interested in you because of your looks, that your looks are being used to signify status to others – and you couldn't even really complain about it to regular people because they wouldn't be able to feel sorry for you. For this reason, I've always found dating attractive men to be easier than dating a man more on my level, because attractive men are already comfortable in their own looks and they don't need to prove to the world that they've done well by securing a knockout girlfriend. Instead, they're happy to date women who are less attractive than them but who they find more intellectually stimulating, because that proves that they have depth.

Beautiful people also have the tiring tasks of minimising their beauty for other people's comfort, and having to constantly let people down without seeming impolite. It's almost like their looks don't belong to them and instead exist in the public realm, where they have the power to make people feel so many different ways about themselves.

Several times, I have asked my friend what the best thing is about being beautiful. Each time, she tries to explain it to me, but to this day I'm still not sure what her answer is. I'll just watch her as she speaks, fascinated by her bone structure and not taking in a single word.

One day, I asked her what the *worst* thing about being beautiful is. She looked at me with her big blue eyes and lamented that the worst thing was that, when a man broke up with her, she knew it was because of her personality.

I did agree that that was tough – at least when a man ended things with me, I could blame my teeny tiny boobs. The kids I used to babysit all have bigger boobs than me now, and I'm furious about it. When I was a pre-pubescent teenager, I wanted boobs so badly. I used to think about what it would be like to walk around with them and what I'd look like in certain outfits. When my friends started developing theirs, I waited patiently for my turn to come, and it never did. I couldn't believe it – everywhere I looked people were growing boobs with ease, and all I ever got was two puffy nipples and three hairs that grow out of them every other month.

And to think, some women get more than they need! Every day I see women walking around with uncomfortably large tits, and I think, *All I need to be satisfied is just a tiny bit off the sides, if they could only spare some.*

I'll admit, I am sometimes insecure about the way I look. I definitely spend way too much time lamenting what I was given.

But I'm also too squeamish for plastic surgery, and too lazy to stick to a strict regimen of facials and spray tans and putting together outfits that highlight my attributes. So instead I try to be thankful for what I've got, which is absolutely appreciated. Honestly, I'm happy just to be alive and to be able to experience my time on Earth in a healthy body.

And so, yes, if it's going on the record, then I suppose I have accepted myself, and most of the time I don't mind looking the way I do. I actually think how I look gives me a unique insight into the human condition. I've always felt that my satisfactory but not extraordinary appearance has given me a certain freedom to fly under the radar, which means I can observe people as they really are – as they're rarely trying to impress me or have sex with me. At least, not at first – wait until they hear my great anecdote/witty put-down!

And I have managed to do just fine with what I have. I've even been told by men who have loved me that I'm beautiful. So I think looks are just whatever you want them to be. If someone likes you enough, they'll put the effort into deciding you're beautiful, and that's actually quite a compliment.

When Gerard posited the idea of me going on this date with Jack, I wasn't sure. I didn't feel like I was ready to meet anyone new. I felt broken and raw from my last relationship and was determined to be unhappy.

But Gerard wouldn't take no for an answer, and a casual double date was set up for that weekend.

I arrived at the pub with Gerard and his girlfriend in the afternoon. Jack was already there. He was one of the most handsome men I'd ever seen, so I decided that, actually, maybe I *was* ready. I bought myself a white wine – a drink that, when given to women who are poised on top of an emotional mountain with happiness on one side and sadness on the other, risks tipping them to either side with each sip, and you never know which side you might land on.

We all sat around for hours, drinking and talking and, to my surprise, I was coming off quite well. I hadn't got to the crux of being truly drunk yet, which is usually when all my troubles start.

I know some people who are allergic to alcohol and break out into angry hives because of it. While I don't break out into hives, my reaction to alcohol is just as unpleasant. See, I have all these thoughts in my head that I don't say when I'm sober. But when I drink, I become confident enough to share them.

After a while, we decided that we'd go to a stand-up comedy gig at which Gerard would be performing. I wasn't supposed to be performing at this particular show, but when we arrived I ended up getting talked into it by the guy running the room. It's all a bit of a blur, but I vaguely remember thinking that maybe this could be good. Jack could watch me do comedy, he would see me being funny and he might even be the one guy who can get hard from laughing. What could possibly go wrong?

I cannot stress enough how much of a horrific disaster it was. It was only when I got up onstage and could barely see that I realised how drunk I was. I was rude and aggressive to the audience and, on top of that, I forgot my jokes. I kept looking into the faces in the crowd, and I could tell they could see how drunk I was and were pissed off. I had to be talked down from the stage by the MC, who felt sorry for me.

I walked back over to the group and Jack was very nice about it all. He could see I was mortified and he assured me that he wouldn't base his assessment of me on this gig.

It was then that all the emotion I'd been suppressing started to well up. (Blame the white wine.) I missed my ex-boyfriend, I missed my parents (perhaps because I had drunk myself into a childlike state) and I just wanted to go home and sit on the couch and eat hot chips with sauce, alone. I could feel the heat rising into my face and, before I knew it, I began crying in front of Jack. Thinking that it couldn't possibly get worse, I mumbled some excuse – what that was, I really couldn't tell you – went to sit down on what I thought was a chair, and found myself folded in half inside one of those round green bins that are large enough to fit a whole girl in them.

So thanks to Jack for being cool about all of that. It means a lot to me that you still occasionally like some of my Instagram posts.

Sport

I love going to the football, because you get to eat like a tradie and scream for no reason – two things I want to do every day but can't, as it's been explained to me that such behaviour is 'annoying' and I will develop 'bowel cancer'.

I find the concept of sport very relaxing, because it typically pits people of relatively comparable strength and ability against each other and, within a particular time frame, we usually know who has won and who has lost. There's a fairness, or at least an attempt at fairness, that doesn't exist in the real world. (It's interesting that the idea of a 'fair and level playing field' in society is considered so outrageous to some of the very people who insist on it in sport.)

It has recently dawned on me how important referees are in sport, and how little they have to gain from it. They take on the job, knowing that no one will ever have a poster of them on their wall, nor will a movie ever be made about the difficult decisions they've had to make. I've never heard of a big-breasted woman falling over herself to talk to a referee, and they aren't ever papped hanging out with the players. They're tantalisingly close to the sporting heroes of the world, yet I doubt a boy has ever boasted to his school friends about his dad's profession as a referee – in fact, I imagine it's got the same stink to it as a staunch lefty admitting their dad is a cop or votes Nationals.

Referees get none of the glory but a lot of the criticism. Does anyone suffer more disrespect than a ref? At the end of the game, depending on whether you're on the winning or losing side, the referees have either done their job adequately, or they are absolute dogs and should be dead.

These refs are clearly so passionate about the game that they've become experts in it, yet they aren't allowed to appear partial to one side, even though they of all people have the most appreciation for how the game was played. It's verging on priesthood in a way. In fact, did you know that referees have to take a vow of celibacy in order to pass their final referee exam? Okay, that's not true – but I bet you believed it.

Yet, for all the flack that referees cop, if a sport were to dismiss all human referees and instead let a computer referee make the decisions with digital precision, all hell would break loose. If it weren't for that element of human error, what would people talk about and fight over all week until the next game? Referees aren't just there to facilitate the game; they're there to act as circuit breakers, so people can blame them instead of the players.

I was at the football with my friends not long ago, sitting a row back from a large group of young, quite obviously private-school boys. It was the sleeveless puffer vests and complete lack of shame about the privileges of cumulative wealth that gave them away.

These types of private-school boys always seem to love their dads in a way that isn't in any way cute or relatable. Meanwhile, their dads probably stay out until 11 pm on weeknights trying to see how much they can drink before spewing on their ties. I used to think private-school boys like this wanted girls to call them 'Daddy' in bed to make them feel dominant and powerful, but I've pivoted into thinking that they just want to be reminded of their actual dads. Any opportunity to discuss their father and his future investments. Even while thrusting away, there's no reason he can't impress upon his lover just how impressive his dad is. 'Daddy? Why, yes, he does have his own parking spot in the city!'

These boys at the footy seemed like they were letting off a bit of steam, no doubt needing some relief from the pressures of living at home in their parents' architect-designed mansions while they saved up enough money for a deposit on a house they would buy at age twenty-three.

I don't want you to think I'm man-bashing here – I love men. But these aren't men; they're Country Road bags running off the fumes of their dads' Mercedes-Benzes. They're the sort who start wars in the Middle East, and do nothing but move other people's money around their whole lives. By age forty, they won't be able to come unless they've paid a woman to crush their scrotum with a high heel. I know it sounds harsh, and I know not *all* private-school boys are like that, obviously – but, my god, I've met so many of them that *are* like that, I'm happy to piss off a few of the good ones as collateral damage.

As I sat behind these boys – about fifteen of them – I became fascinated by their dynamic and began watching them instead of the football game. I even began to feel sorry for the few who were not as alpha as the others, and who probably just wanted to watch the game in peace as opposed to being part of this undulating human sea of white skin, sandy-coloured hair and homophobic slurs.

I quickly figured out that they were not loyal to each other in the slightest and, in fact, would attack each other in order to avoid being a target. To protect themselves from being made fun of or called a 'pussy', they had to instead point at someone else and make them the subject of a put-down. It seemed like a very stressful situation to be in.

'You need to go to the toilet? You're a fucking pussy, mate,' one said, before surreptitiously looking around to see if he'd pulled it off.

The boy who had just had this accusation levelled at him hesitated, and another boy a few seats away stepped in on his behalf, either out of solidarity or merely pure self-interest. 'Why are you so obsessed with him going to the toilet, you gay cunt?' To which he received a huge laugh and a round of high-fives.

The boy who initiated the exchange retreated. He would need to gather himself before attempting anything like that again.

At last, their team scored a try and they all begun bellowing like wild animals into the cold night.

'Fucking yessss, boys, ow ow owwwwww!' one shouted and the others joined in.

One boy, getting so excited by all the yelling, started roaring louder and louder until he lost control and was betrayed by his very own vocal cords, which turned his previously manly roar into a high-pitched squeal. His eyes widened and he could tell he was in for it. They all converged on him in a barrage of insults, the loudest coming from the boy who had lost the battle from earlier. This barrage lasted around three minutes. I noticed that the squealer didn't speak much for the rest of the night.

In my later schooling years, I went to a public high school that offered placements for kids who displayed academic or sporting excellence, which meant it was considered a selective school and so we competed against private schools. Let me be clear, I was not there for any kind of academic or sporting reasons – I just lived in the catchment area so they had to take me in, much to the chagrin of the more-talented students.

I went to a few of the rugby games our school played against the private schools. The private-school kids would chant 'Your dad works for my dad' at us over and over until the game started. Then the chant would taper off somewhat as they watched their team get destroyed by players who lived in suburbs the private-school kids would never step foot in, like Marsden, Beenleigh and Browns Plains.

The private-school kids would always cry that it wasn't fair that they had to compete against our school, because we had players who were genetically more gifted – that is, players who were from places like Tonga and Samoa, and had more natural agility and strength than the chinless private-school boys.

What *was* fair to them, though, was that they would all go on to own property and receive jobs from their friends' dads without having to bother with all that irksome 'interview process' stuff.

Now back to the private-school boys sitting in front of me at the football. Towards the end of the night, the game nearly over, a boy with rat-like features who hadn't done anything in a while threw his beer up into the air. It landed all over a couple of middle-aged Indian men sitting a few rows in front. The boys began cackling and hitting each other on the back, when the friend I was with, who is truly gargantuan in size, tapped the little rat boy on the shoulder.

'Mate, what the fuck was that?' my friend said. 'Go and apologise to those men now.'

The boy, rolling his eyes cockily to his friends, started to turn around in his seat. 'What the fuck are y—' he began, before clocking the entirety of my friend's stature.

Without another word, he scuttled off down the concrete steps, profusely apologising to the men he'd spilt beer on, while furtively glancing up at my large friend to make sure he was satisfied.

Thank you to sport for occasionally being there to facilitate dunking on people who really need to be dunked on.

Santa

What I'm about to say is really going to break the mould, but I loved Santa when I was a kid. I spent a lot of time thinking about him and what I'd say if I ever got to meet him. Nothing sycophantic, of course; I wanted him to respect me and see me as an equal – maybe even as a friend?

My faith in Santa was tested again and again by my cousins, who would regularly taunt, 'If he's real, then how is he "everywhere at once"?' Which never made sense to me. I wasn't there believing in a *normal* man who could do all of these incredible things – I believed in a real man who possessed magical qualities, obviously. And who could trust their cousins anyway? Especially after finding out that they also had cousins on their other side who you'd never met. I always found that fact shocking – you'd be hanging out with your cousins on Christmas

Day or whatever, and the next day they'd all be off to do the same song and dance with a whole different bunch of kids.

My cousins weren't the only ones trying to sow seeds of doubt. I'd heard the playground rumours, but my desire to feel that there was some magical world running parallel to mine kept me true to my beliefs.

Then, one Christmas, I saw my mum using the same ribbon as the one that was on Santa's gifts, and I decided to confront her. Frankly, I was furious that she'd made such an obvious gaffe. I may have only been five, but, come on, it's like she wanted to be caught.

The surprising thing was that she actually crumbled and gave a full confession almost straight away. I started crying. I didn't actually want to know! I wanted her to give me some counterargument that could explain the ribbon away. Who gives in to pressure from a five-year-old?

It was an important lesson for me: never ask a question you don't actually want the answer to. For example, when you ask a friend if you were too drunk the night before, you really need to be okay with them telling you that, yes, you were. And maybe you shouldn't put your friend in the position where they have to lie and say, 'No, no, you were fine.'

I must admit that once I learnt the truth from my mum, it took me a few years to admit to my dad that I knew Santa wasn't real. Because of my parents' divorce, I often got to be two different versions of myself and play out two different realities.

With my mum, I was the smug know-it-all who had figured out the truth, and with my dad, I was the naïve innocent who could once again get to experience the magic of Christmas and Santa. I also thought that if I told my dad I didn't believe in Santa, our special time would be ruined, and I wouldn't get to watch the one-man show he would perform just for me, where he would make footprints in talcum powder and put out biscuits and carrots for Santa and his reindeers. I gave some truly Oscar-winning performances pretending to believe it all.

I have found myself doing similar performances with men I'm dating, where I'll go along with something I know is a lie, because I worry that if I tell them the truth, I'll embarrass them and break the magic.

As an adult, I love asking other people what their relationship to Santa was like when they were younger and how they found out he wasn't real. I think these questions can reveal a lot about someone's character and early home life.

I've noticed that every time I ask these questions, I get one of two reactions: either they politely laugh, assuming I'm just being frivolous, or they claim that they don't really remember.

To get the ball rolling, I'll start talking about my own fascination with the concept of Santa and how I feel it relates to my family dynamic, specifically how I think it helped shape my idea of authority. Because, for me, Santa provided an important stepping stone to learning how to gather evidence, put forward my case, and question people in charge. I think it's good for kids to realise that there are some things that don't add up, and they should feel comfortable to prod and push their parents when they think something's awry. It's also important for parents to assess just how well the kids have done their research and reward them with the truth. I suppose you could say working out the truth about Santa is a kid's first piece of investigative journalism.

Also, Santa was the first man I loved and trusted who would turn out to betray me. I've come to believe that you learn a lot from the men who hurt you, and I'd like to think that my experience with Santa made me wise to the fact that a man in a powerful position might not be all he's cracked up to be, and that his status could be a part of a power structure that simply isn't real. Because of this, I think I've managed to sidestep a lot of unwanted male attention in my industry. I don't think I possess the ability to reflect the love and importance a lot of men in power feel for themselves back at them, which means, in terms of sex pests, I've mostly been left alone.

Once I'm about halfway through this often stoned and drunken spiel, I can see the other person start to realise that I am actually giving them full permission to tell a long, self-involved story about their childhood. This is of course unless we've all been doing cocaine, in which case I didn't really have to probe in the first place.

When they realise I genuinely want to know their answer, they start to recall their childhood Santa story with exceptional clarity, despite having previously laughed it off. It's my belief that my insistence that I will actually listen gives them the energy to truly engage with the question.

This belief was initially sparked by a revelation I conceived of one night after a particularly bad dinner party. There was a girl in attendance who I could tell was impressed by her own ability to ask great questions. The problem was, she wasn't particularly interested in the answers.

One particular exchange left an impression on me.

'Do you think having a background in social work has been helpful or detrimental for your new project?' she'd asked someone, eyes flashing with self-congratulation for having remembered the person's background in social work.

'I'm not sure if I've consciously made that connection,' replied the other person, looking a bit bamboozled by her sudden interest in their work, 'but I think fundamentally coming from a field you're more aware of—'

'I'd love to do social work; we're thinking of volunteering over Christmas,' the girl sang out, having in her mind just completed a perfect back-and-forth.

I watched on, amazed at how oblivious she was to this downfall in her personality, which was by every other standard quite dazzling.

I do think people forget how exhausting it can be to answer a question truthfully and well – so if you're going to ask one, make sure, for your sake and theirs, that you really want the answer. I often try to remind myself that when you ask someone a question, be it an interesting one or not, you're asking them to be vulnerable and to expend energy in answering it, so the least you can do is listen to the answer.

I'm sorry to harp on about this, but this also plays into another theory I have about celebrity interviews, which I personally believe are terrible nowadays. I think that this is due in part to the fact that the person conducting interviews in the modern media landscape is more on a quest for fame themselves and not so much interested in their interview subject as they are in their own fledgling (or flailing) career.

I have another friend, who unfortunately wasn't at that dinner party, but who is incredible at bringing out the gold in anyone. She can get to the most interesting thing about anybody within five minutes, and that person will leave the interaction feeling like they're the greatest storyteller of all time. (They're not. My friend is just great at asking questions and then listening to the reply.)

I think that's what great interviewers used to do. They were so good at making curiosity look easy that other people saw it and thought, *This looks like a good way to become famous*, not realising that we watched those interviews for what they could bring out in the celebrity, not just for the interviewer's proximity to fame.

So when people initially back away from engaging in my Santa chat, I completely understand why. But excitingly for them, I'm actually very interested in Santa. Once I convince them of this, I'm often rewarded with an insightful story from their childhood.

I have a friend who is Jewish and she claims that, having not grown up being told about Santa, she was always intrigued by her friends at school who believed in him. She remembers feeling very adult and like she had an important role to play by not spoiling it for them by exposing the secret. There was also a sense of benevolence that came from this responsibility.

Because of this early experience, she feels strangely protective when she sees a group of people who believe in something she can't identify with. Even now, if she senses a group of people strongly believe in something, she feels like the kindest thing to do is to let them go ahead and believe it. She's been like that for as long as she can remember, and up until I asked her about Santa, she'd never made the connection.

Thank you to Santa, for being a great topic of discussion between me and others, and for being one of the main reasons I try to listen to people's answers rather than pat myself on the back for having asked a good question – something I was definitely guilty of for many years.

crazyhorny64

Years ago, I stumbled on a YouTube comment left on one of my videos by a man with the username 'crazyhorny64'. He'd commented, 'you are a very bad woman'.

It piqued my interest – because I am, but how did he know?

In general, I don't read online comments. I know people say that, and often they're lying, but I don't. There's something so shocking about seeing something mean written about you – it's the same feeling you get when you hear a friend has said something nasty about you behind your back. I don't know why it's shocking. *Everyone* bad-mouths another person at least once in a while. There has to be some coping mechanism in your brain that convinces you that, even though you might talk shit about others, no one else is doing the same to you. Mean comments are proof that people *do* talk about you, and not in a nice way, and that's very confronting no matter how evolved you might be.

But that's not the only reason I don't like to look at comments. I am also repelled by the nice ones, which often have the effect of embarrassing me. Sometimes I feel waves of shame about forcing my face and voice out into the public and pretty much begging for acceptance and praise. I've had moments onstage where the crowd are laughing and enjoying themselves, and I have this overwhelming feeling of guilt, almost like an out-of-body experience, where I realise how ridiculous it is that I've insisted people gather into a dark room to watch me spout off under the spotlight.

However, despite my natural aversion to looking at online comments, sometimes it's unavoidable. Maybe the comment has popped up on my screen and I haven't been able to cancel out of it quickly enough; or I'm drunk and alone in a hotel room at 3 am, looking to have my feelings hurt. And there it is: a perfect stranger's opinion about me. And suddenly I have to know everything about them.

After I read crazyhorny64's comment, I typed his username into Google and very easily found an identical one being used on a forum that was primarily populated by men who are in relationships with sex dolls. After a bit more sleuthing, I confirmed it was the same man, and then spent hours looking at his sordid little love life.

I want to interject here and acknowledge that I understand there are some men who benefit greatly from owning a sex doll. For example, there are men with physical disabilities or behavioural disorders who, due to a lack of confidence, often find it difficult to meet women or be in relationships. And then there are men who wear T-shirts with funny slogans, who have a lot of confidence, but are also unable to meet women.

Perusing this forum, I was struck by the fact that these men weren't using these dolls simply as a receptacle, but were forming loving, meaningful relationships with them. As a woman who lacks the typical measurements considered sexually desirable, I've always taken comfort in the idea that a woman with a nice personality or a good sense of humour is just as likely to find a mate as a woman who is conventionally attractive. So it was disheartening to see these men were all completely in love with what are essentially women they can rinse out. I also noted that nearly all the dolls had names like 'Crystal', 'Tami' or 'Delilah', which made me nostalgic for the old days where a man wouldn't be in charge of naming anything except his boat.

Not only did these men seem to have genuine feelings for these dolls, but they also did what normal couples do. There was a man who posted a photo of his doll sitting perfectly still with her arms outstretched. The caption read, 'She's finally letting me pick the movie.' I can't be sure, but I think I could see the *Star Wars* crawl text reflected off her latex skin.

Then of course there was crazyhorny64. He was a pretty active member of the group and had recently posted a photo of him taking his sex doll, named 'April', out to get her hair cut. I had assumed that one of the perks of having a sex doll would be that their hair didn't grow, so you wouldn't have to suffer the indignity of taking her to a very public salon, but, from what I could gather, that's part of the fun.

In his post, he claimed that the hairdresser was very understanding of their situation, and some of the other customers were very supportive and even had a lot of questions for him! He ended by expressing a bit of annoyance that, after April's haircut, she 'insisted' on going shopping, and that he, being the man, was forced to pick up the bill!

I suppose what I'm trying to say is that this man had a girlfriend who was made from a plastic mould and was incapable of sentience and thought. He could have projected any traits he wanted onto this object, essentially creating his dream woman. And apparently, his idea of a perfect woman is a shallow creature who loves shopping and relies on money from her hard-working man to pay for her lifestyle. I guess he was just desperate to play the role of a man encumbered by the demands of his girlfriend; that way he could roll his eyes and claim 'women be shopping'.

I was satisfied that, no matter what I did to try and make him like me, I wouldn't ever be a good-enough woman for crazyhorny64.

So thank you to crazyhorny64, for this realisation about online critics: sometimes people's feelings about you are justified. But sometimes the universe has, for whatever reason, decided to throw you in the path of a man with an internet connection and a girlfriend who would melt if left in a Westfield shopping centre carpark.

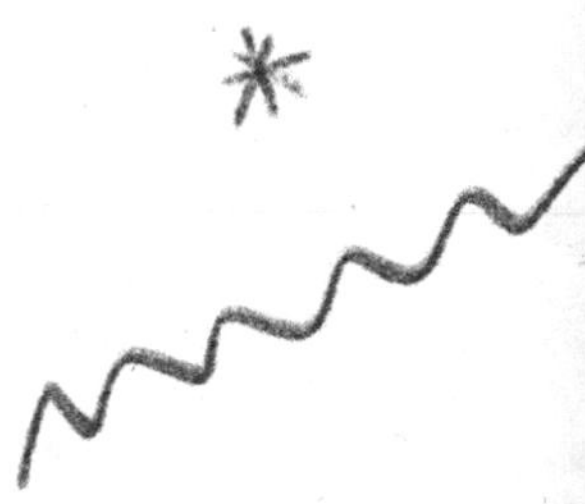

Rachel

Rachel was dangerous, even at seven years old, which was when we first became friends. She was a sort of troublemaking shaman, who could figure out how best to ruin an adult's day using whatever was on hand. With a casual glance at the house and backyard, she'd pick three items – a barrel, foam balls from the inside of a beanbag, and a jar of honey – and create chaos.

This was perfect for me, because the ensuing chaos was never *my* doing, and I've always been strangely drawn to chaos that's outside of my control – or, at least, that's unable to be pinned on me. I never want to be in the epicentre of it or be directly responsible for it, but I've always been more than happy to stand on the edges and look in.

I've had this strange attraction to chaos as long as I can remember. At the age of six, months after the death of my beloved pet mouse, Lisa Marie, my mum let me pick out another one at the pet shop. Within two days, it had given birth to six babies. I knew I should have immediately told Mum, but I didn't, because I had a sick curiosity about what would happen. Instead, I kept the box of mice secreted away under my bed, secure in the knowledge that *technically* I wasn't doing anything wrong. I was just letting nature take its course.

After another couple of weeks, some of those babies had babies, and, within a month, I had forty or so mice. I couldn't help but look on in glee at the madness of all the moving mice. So many of them writhing around, and all because of me. I enjoyed the idea of this box of churning, unauthorised life unfurling without any direct input from me, yet I was able to peer into it whenever I wanted.

Three months after the initial purchase, my mum caught me holding eight of the baby mice at one time and it was all over. That was the end of my reign over my little rodent kingdom. She took the box and disposed of them. I'm not exactly sure what happened to them all; I want to believe she took them back to the pet shop, where they found loving homes for all sixty-four mice, but there was a creek nearby and I can only assume that was their final resting place.

Rachel was sort of like my box of mice, in that I wasn't directly responsible for the trouble she caused, but I certainly didn't do anything to stop it. I wasn't a naturally naughty child and I'm not a naturally naughty adult, but I can be talked into almost anything if it's fun enough – and unfortunately the fun stuff is usually the stuff you're not supposed to do.

One day when Rachel was over at my place, she grabbed a bottle of Morning Fresh dishwashing liquid and a skipping rope, and created a 'slippery slide' on the roof by squeezing the dishwashing liquid all over it and spraying it with a hose. She then told me to get onto the roof and hold on tight to the skipping rope as she pulled me this way and that. Both of us took turns tugging each other along the hot tin roof covered in suds, every now and then careening out of control towards the edge, where we'd just manage to stop ourselves in time before we could fall off. After we'd had about four or five turns each, my mum came outside and caught us in the act. She stared at us open-mouthed, rendered truly speechless and unable to understand how we'd rigged such an effective death trap in the twenty minutes she'd left us unattended.

Later that afternoon, as we lounged around in timeout, I asked Rachel what she wanted to be when she grew up.

'A sex machine,' she said, after no thought whatsoever.

'Oh,' I replied.

Being friends with Rachel felt like being friends with a snake or a shark or some other animal that you couldn't relax around. I was always worried that she'd turn on me. But, taking in all my options, which was Cindy across the road who used to incessantly ask me to smell her finger, Rachel was the best I had. And at least she wasn't boring. Plus, if I'm going to be honest, she was a fan of the five-fingered discount and would regularly steal coins from her mum's purse to buy us both lollies.

Rachel and I would often hang out together after school, alternating between her place and mine. One thing I've observed during the years of going over to someone's house for a play or a sleepover is that some parents really adhere to the idea of their kid's friends being 'guests' in their house, and would bend over backwards to put on a little show for you. It was divine; suddenly, you went from being a nothing kid to a little princess being waited on hand and foot. That kind of treatment was easy to get used to. There was one girl I stayed friends with for longer than I should have, because I adored the little trays laden with treats her mum would bring out to the pool with a smile. There was none of that at my house, or Rachel's house – neither of our mums bothered with this veneer of niceness. I didn't love getting yelled at by someone else's mum, but on the flip side I didn't have to be embarrassed when my mum did it to Rachel. I do, however, remember the shocking day I was forced to participate in Saturday-morning chores with Rachel and the rest of her family, and thinking that this was, actually, too far.

My Year Three teacher was a blonde toad of a woman, who wore big chunky gold jewellery, had lipstick lines that would always form in the folds of her lips, and hated me. I couldn't understand what she didn't like about me. I didn't feel that I was troublesome or even stood out in any real way at all. What confused me even more is that she liked Rachel, when it seemed like public knowledge that, of the two of us, I was the good one.

No one believes kids when they tell you that their teachers don't like them. I think people assume that when you're a teacher, part of the job description includes trying your best to at least act as if you like your students. I can understand why some teachers might not like certain students though – children tend to mimic their parents' annoying behaviour, plus they lack boundaries and sometimes piss themselves.

When I have an issue with someone, it's generally because of something tangible, like a difference in political beliefs, a romantic rift or, in my weaker moments, career jealousy. That's what makes it so hard for adults to really believe kids when they tell them their teacher doesn't like them – the idea of an adult having enough common ground with a child in order to form a genuine beef seems a bit silly.

Looking back, I wonder if this teacher had even tried to act as if she liked me or, even worse, had tried and just couldn't. I know that teaching is a hard job – the pay isn't good enough and there's a lot of pressure – but I believe that teachers should be reminded that when they have an irrational dislike of a student, it really sticks with us.

My Year Two teacher loved me, but hated a boy called Doug. One day a girl in our class came to school, her hair teeming with lice. As the teacher lifted up her hair with a ruler to inspect the infestation, Doug shouted, 'Ew! Nits!'

The teacher turned around and spat, 'Look at you! You've got disgusting warts all over your elbow and you're fat!' After which he and the whole class fell silent.

I bumped into Doug years later at a bar somewhere in the city. Struggling to make conversation, I brought up that incident and asked him if he remembered it. He went quiet for a moment before he said, yes, he remembered it well.

I recently came across a similar example when I did a day's work in a writers' room for a children's TV show. As the show was about school, naturally we writers and producers started discussing our own schooling experiences. Eventually, the discussion came around to bullying and nicknames, and one of the show's creators launched into a story.

He told us that when he was younger, he was a lot chubbier. After he said this, he paused and looked around, as if expecting all of us to congratulate him on what a svelte figure he now cut. When no one said anything, he continued. He said that, as well as being chubby, he also played the tuba, which didn't exactly help matters. I wasn't surprised to hear that. The sight of a rotund boy waddling along already conjures the sound of a tuba – and he went and actually played one! How did they decide who played what instrument in that school? I shudder to think that they simply looked around the room and assigned instruments to kids who looked like they were up to the task.

Anyway, he told us that there had been one afternoon when he'd been running late to band practice. He'd bustled into the classroom, put his tuba together and sat down in his seat. The teacher looked up and, with a smirk, asked, 'Why are you so late, Beach Ball?'

And the whole class erupted into laughter.

'Kids called me "Beach Ball" for the entirety of high school!' he said, chortling heartily to show us that it was all in the past now and, besides, look at him now, he was about to have his very own TV show.

We all chuckled at the anecdote and resumed swapping stories and working on episode structures.

About an hour later, we broke for lunch. As we were grazing on different snacks in various bowls, I went for a bowl of chips on the other side of the table, but couldn't quite reach it. Deciding to have some light-hearted fun, I called out, 'Hey, Beach Ball! Pass us those chips, will ya?'

I was met with complete silence. The creator looked down at his lap, obviously really upset. That shit never goes away.

Anyway, back to the teacher who hated me.

One afternoon, after lunch break, she came up to me and said, 'I need to talk to you.'

She walked me outside, presumably so she could speak to me the way she really wanted to, and told me I was a thief and should be ashamed of myself; that I was so stupid for thinking I could get away with it.

I stood there, genuinely confused. I couldn't figure out what the fuck she was on about.

She continued to scream at me, spit flying wildly out of her mouth. As I tried to protest, her eyes became even more gleeful – oh, to finally have a reason to hate me!

Eventually, I managed to get out of her just what it was that I had supposedly done. I was accused of stealing five Goosebumps books from the bag of another student, who had brought them in for show and tell. She said there were witnesses to me being in the classroom, where the bag had been, at lunchtime.

'Yes ...' I cautiously began. 'Me and Rachel came up to get our hats, but I promise I didn't steal any books.'

She scoffed. 'I know you like Goosebumps books. I've seen you reading them.'

Even to an eight-year-old, this seemed like very flimsy evidence. Of course I liked Goosebumps books. I also liked Milo, boogie boarding and forgetting to bring my lunchbox to school.

I'll never forget the way she marched me back into class and said to the boy who owned the books, 'Becky stole them, but she won't admit to it,' or how the entire class sat there staring at me. I will never forget the sense of injustice I felt. If anything, it rankles even more now – at least these days if I'm being accused of doing something bad, it's generally because I've actually done it.

I couldn't make sense of it. I was in a funk all afternoon. The worst thing was that, having not actually committed the crime I was accused of, I didn't even have a good Goosebumps book to lose myself in.

That evening, I finally told my mum what had happened.

'If you stole them, just tell me. Because if I go in there and defend you and then find out you did it, you'll be in so much trouble,' she said.

I solemnly swore I was innocent and my mum believed me, which was very kind considering what had happened with the sixty-four mice.

The next day, she put on a nice skirt and a bold lip and went to school to defend my honour. She told the teacher to never speak to me like that again or she'd make a formal complaint. I remember there being a lot of yelling, my mum at the teacher and vice versa. My mum was young, and hot, and only recently did I piece it together that that might have been the reason my toadlike teacher hated me.

Despite her best efforts, my teacher couldn't pin the crime on me, and after that she more or less had to drop the whole thing. Time passed and things went back to normal. I barely thought about the incident, except on the odd occasion when I'd notice my classmates move their things out of my reach. I was, in their eyes, a criminal who'd got off on a technicality.

But that sort of thing didn't bother me much. Even as a kid, I could sense that this stuff and those people only sort of mattered. Besides, it was nearly school holidays, and Rachel's family had just got an above-ground swimming pool.

One afternoon over the holidays, Rachel and I were sitting in the back of my mum's blue Ford Laser, eating slices of fresh bread from the plastic bag Mum had hurled through the window before running off to complete more errands.

Rachel turned to me and said, 'Do you want to know something?'

Then she opened her schoolbag and pulled out the five Goosebumps books I'd been accused of taking.

Enough time had passed that I couldn't precisely remember how hurt I'd felt at the time of the false accusation, so I wasn't even mad at Rachel. I just sort of nodded and said something about how it was unfair that I had taken all the blame.

She had this grotesque smile on her face as she opened her palm to reveal eighty warm cents that she'd stolen from her mum's purse. A bribe. She told me I could have the money if I kept her secret, and to this day I can't remember if I took it or not.

Thank you to Rachel for the many years of friendship, the lollies, and the reminder that if you play with snakes or sharks, you will get bit!

Pam

As I mentioned earlier, my mum was a country singer and musician who would regularly play at music festivals. Sometimes I'd stay with my grandma, or a friend's family, but often she would bring me along and hire someone to look after me while she was performing.

When I was around six years old, my mum hired a woman called Pam to look after me during these festivals. When I asked her years later how she had found Pam, she said she didn't know, which I can believe.

I remember Pam being quite elderly and refined, with a glass of white wine permanently attached to her right hand. My mum said she was actually only about forty and just had a drinking problem.

Kids never know when adults have drinking problems. One of my best friends in primary school had a dad with a drinking problem and we didn't know, we just thought he was really fun. (He used to give a bunch of us lifts home after school, and he'd play this great game in the car where he'd let us take our seatbelts off and then he'd careen around the back streets, taking corners at breakneck speed, and we'd go flying around the back seat, screaming with joy.) When you're young, you can't imagine what adults are trying to achieve by drinking, because you're either in the middle of – or still yet to experience – the pain you'll eventually want to forget.

There was a time in my mid-twenties when I had started touring with other comedians around Australia, performing at theatres and RSLs every night. On one of those trips, I met an older male comedian who was sober and had been for some time. One morning, having written myself off the night before, I crawled into the tour van, nursing a plastic bag in case I needed to vomit. I jokingly mentioned to him and the others that I wouldn't mind going to AA. Perhaps it was semi-jokingly, if I'm being honest – I wasn't really serious about it, but I did kind of want to know what the others thought of me.

'Noooo, you're fine. You don't need to do that,' is what I expected the others to say in response. Instead, there was this kind of unanimous group reaction that seemed to imply that I should definitely think about it.

Hours later, after we'd checked into our motel, I was trying to get half an hour of much-needed rest before the show that night, when the sober comedian sent me a text.

'Hey, as you know, I have some experience with AA, I've been sober for 15 years. Feel free to ask me anything.'

I wrote back, 'What does AA stand for?'

It's odd to me how easily we point the finger at someone drinking too much or always being drunk without really wondering why, when that is in fact what we *should* be asking. That being said, I don't know what had happened in Pam's life that might have precipitated her drinking problem. I have to present her to you based on the impressions I formed as a child, and I'm not even entirely sure what they were. I used to hate Pam, but now that I'm older I don't know if she was really as bad as I thought she was. I can barely remember anything she said to me, which is frustrating because I'm afraid there's still some Pam in me. Isn't it scary how adults can tell kids things when our brains are still forming, and we can't really tell what's worth keeping or throwing away? Who knows what damaging things you might internalise during this vulnerable time?

It's kind of the same reason I'm a bit wary about what entertainment I consume. I love TV shows and books with bad characters who say deplorable things, because what is the point of art that only reaffirms your worldview? But I do worry that once the characters' thoughts are in my head, my brain won't categorise the information into 'good' or 'bad' and instead just recognise them as 'valid'. Sometimes when I say things, I can't be sure if it's how I actually feel or whether I'm just repeating something I heard somewhere. I might even be spouting off the opinion of Cruella de Vil. For that reason, I try to never be too tethered to my thoughts or ideas and always welcome counterarguments. For all I know, the thoughts I have might not be my own, and so not worth defending.

I do remember that Pam would promise me things and never deliver. Like the time she told me we'd get ice cream if I was good, and then acted confused when I brought up my impeccable behaviour hours later. This incident was particularly sinister in my opinion, because she knew that it wasn't a big-enough crime for me to report back to my mum. It's one thing when someone lets you down because they've honestly dropped the ball, but when they let you down because they think they can get away with it, it feels personal. But maybe I'm projecting my adult assessment onto that scenario – it might have just been because she was too drunk to drive me to the ice cream shop. See, look at me not being tethered to my thoughts.

Mum stopped letting Pam look after me when, under Pam's supervision, I backflipped into a pool and cracked my head open, and Pam was too intoxicated to notice. I remember the pool filling with my bright-red blood while my mum swam around in it, trying to keep my head above water.

But years later, when I was around nine or ten, my mum and her band were asked at short notice to open for a singer from America, and she was desperate enough to ask Pam to watch me backstage.

The singer had been quite famous in the early 1960s. He had a few songs that you probably wouldn't know and one that you probably would. He would come to Australia every couple of years and perform shows at various RSLs. Just like at concerts today, the old people would politely nod along to the songs from his back catalogue, then lose it at the one song they recognised.

I knew that this gig was a big deal. Usually, if my mum performed at an RSL, I would have to just sit underneath one of the plastic tables, playing and drinking pink lemonade until it was time to go home. But on this occasion, she had her own dressing room in the special downstairs area, right next to the American singer's, where I could wait with Pam.

Pam arrived in the carpark at the same time as we did, only briefly glancing at the scar on my forehead, her only acknowledgment of our previous time together. Then she sat with me while my mum and her band did their warmup and rehearsal.

Later, while the audience was filing in (they give them a good hour or so to get seated in those places), we all sat together in the dressing room. Shortly before my mum went onstage, the one-hit wonder from America came in and introduced himself.

He had a bouffant hairdo and a fancy belt buckle and was very polite, the way all Americans are, because I suppose, in their country, if you aren't polite, you might get shot.

I remember being starstruck, even though I had no idea who he was. He remembered my name, said he was so very pleased that we could all be there, and wished my mum luck, also mentioning that anyone was welcome to the drinks in his fridge, which elicited an interested look from Pam. Then my mum and her band left the room to perform their opening set. Pam asked if I wanted to stay in the dressing room or watch the set. As I was halfway through a good book at the time, I chose to stay and eat some of the complimentary crudités.

I didn't have long to enjoy either, though, because a few moments later, the American singer popped his head around the door and asked me if I wanted to see his dressing room. I looked over at Pam, who nodded encouragingly. I didn't actually want to see his dressing room, but I also didn't want to seem impolite. It was the same feeling I'd had when one of my dad's friends showed me his Tamagotchi at a dinner party. I couldn't have cared less about the contraption, but I felt I had to play the role of an excited child.

I followed the singer into his dressing room, which was much bigger than my mum's – and empty. As I gazed around the room, I became aware that the air felt different and his demeanour had noticeably changed. His eyes seemed to soften when he looked at me.

I was examining something on the dresser when I noticed the scent of his cologne getting stronger. He walked up behind me and began cuddling me and rubbing my lower back, while repeating again and again what a pretty girl I was.

Before I had time to understand what was happening, the door opened and Pam stuck her head into the room, causing him to jump away from me and break into a big, toothy American smile.

If I ever catch myself staring at the scar on my head, I always think of Pam for saving me in that moment. Looking back, though, I genuinely don't think she knew what she'd interrupted. I have a feeling she was just looking for those drinks he'd mentioned earlier.

So thank you to Pam for your dedication to the drink. Your unwavering lust for white wine stopped a bad situation from becoming much worse.

The man who fell down the stairs

My friend Sophie and I went on a trip to Europe when we were just a bit too young for it. At least, that's how I felt at the time – I barely knew what I liked or what cultural exploits to even look out for. The whole thing felt like a bit of a blur, and I'd wondered if the experience was wasted on me.

It's always taken me a bit longer to get with the program than most of my friends. Some girls become fully grown women as soon as they graduate from high school. You look down into a packet of Twisties and by the time you look up, they're rustling around inside a bulging handbag searching for the keys to their Suzuki Swift. By the age of twenty-three, they're ready for motherhood and a maroon lip. But not me. I'm thirty-one and I still don't have my driver's licence. And I've never once had a tampon on me when I needed one.

Sophie and I didn't really know what we were doing, but we did like to drink, so one afternoon in Croatia, we found a bar and sat down with the intention of drinking at least five standard drinks each. The downstairs section was a busy restaurant, and upstairs was a large outdoor courtyard. We made our way to the courtyard and found ourselves a table close to the stairs.

Shortly after we'd sat down, two middle-aged couples asked to join us. The only thing I can remember about one of the couples was that the woman had the attitude of an ex-flight attendant who couldn't be bothered smiling politely anymore. But the other couple, whom we spoke to most, were very chatty and engaging. Not to mention that, after travelling with one person for a few months, it doesn't take much to lock in on some new social stimulus. I distinctly remember feeling quite adult in that moment, drinking beers with a couple of middle-aged people, going round for round and pulling it off.

The wife in the more interesting couple seemed very nice, in a 'manager of T2' kind of way. She was inoffensive and warm and seemed to take us seriously, so we instantly liked her.

Her husband was a real estate agent and that checked out completely. His conversation felt more like a one-man show that he'd performed and perfected, in that it didn't require much of our input at all. I don't mind that type of person; it can be relaxing to let them orate to the group while you sit back and chime in when you feel like it, often scoring an easy laugh off all their hard work.

He sat with perfect posture, which is one of my more unpopular pet hates – I often slouch as a way to show people I've just met that I don't think I'm that good. I know it's wrong, verging on insane, to be annoyed by something that's genuinely better for people's health, but there's just something so grating to me about someone who doesn't have the humility to slouch, even just a little bit, at first meeting.

His wife didn't talk as much as he did, and instead alternated between suppressing eye rolls every time he used a word he'd clearly just learnt, reminding him that he was sitting near the top of the stairs and to stop moving around so much, and giving us serious side eye every time he lectured us on the benefits of travelling.

Almost every person who has told me how travelling made them a better person has proved themselves to be an utter dud. Obviously I agree that getting more life experience under your belt will help you become a more well-rounded person, or an extremely effective psychopath, but the idea that travel in and of itself is the best way to do it seems flawed. I suspect the people who travelled back when it was less of a done thing learnt a lot about themselves, as they would have been forced to meet and interact with completely different people just to do simple things, like catch a bus. But nowadays, with all the apps at people's fingertips and the tour groups that schedule you down to the minute, the only lesson people seem to learn from travelling is how to say, 'Do you have a phone charger?' in Spanish.

And don't get me started on people who post pictures of their boarding pass next to their glass of Champagne on social media. What a lame ode to the dull process of travelling. What's next? Posting pictures of your driver's licence? Or a medical certificate that states you are carrying your EpiPen?

As the night wore on, this man continued to completely disprove his point about people bettering themselves by travelling, by saying things like, 'The world is a book and those who don't travel only read a page,' while intermittently disappearing into the bathroom to do lines of coke. Meanwhile, the rest of us committed to getting as drunk as possible.

At one point, sensing the conversation was heading in a direction that didn't involve him, he once again impressed upon me and Sophie the *importance* of travelling, claiming, as his chair edged closer and closer to the top of the stairs, that just this year he'd been to Spain, to Rome, to London—

And in a burst of coke-induced enthusiasm, this man disappeared mid-sentence down an entire flight of stairs. I caught a glimpse of his manic face as he went down and, in that brief moment, he showed so much vulnerability that for the first time that night I found myself liking him.

He and his chair rocketed to the bottom of the stairs and slid along the restaurant floor, coming to a slow stop beside a big family eating an early dinner. Waiters ran to his aid and he angrily shooed them away, like his fall was their fault. He wiggled out of the chair with some difficulty, jumped up and ran back up the stairs, chair in hand, perhaps thinking that the quicker he returned to us, the less chance we had of noticing that he'd fallen down an entire flight of stairs. He settled back into the group, refusing the sympathies of the other couple and his wife, then, without missing a beat, he continued listing the places he'd been to that year. Then he insisted, once again, that we simply *had* to travel.

I remember thinking that if I were to give him advice, it would simply be to not fall down a flight of stairs mid-story.

The really disappointing thing for me and Sophie was that no one really acknowledged what had happened. The others reacted with genuine expressions of concern for him; meanwhile, Sophie and I had just witnessed possibly the funniest thing that we were ever going to see in our lives, and we weren't able to enjoy a second of it. For the next half hour, we were forced to sit there and pretend that everything was normal, and that a fully grown man hadn't just fallen down a flight of stairs mid-boast. It was a huge effort, and our throats and foreheads nearly exploded with the tension from our suppressed laughter.

Eventually we stood up, excused ourselves and walked down the stairs, not daring to look at each other. Then, once we were a safe distance from the bar, we locked eyes and stood there laughing solidly for about ten minutes. The entire walk home, we'd scream every couple of minutes and ask each other if what just happened was real. We kept repeating the phrase 'not normal', because it was the only way to describe what had happened.

I often wonder about that couple, and whether the wife was ever able to respect him again. I suppose true love is watching your spouse topple down a flight of stairs and finding it within yourself to honour the lifelong commitment you made to him.

I want to thank this man for reminding me that, if you stack it hard, it is your responsibility to give permission to those around you to laugh. The only way you can leave that situation without a laugh is if an ambulance is called, but anything less than that, the people around you should be allowed to laugh and laugh and laugh. Otherwise we're just forced to share in your embarrassment. Never be afraid to take your lumps. You fell. We get to laugh. It's the natural order of things.

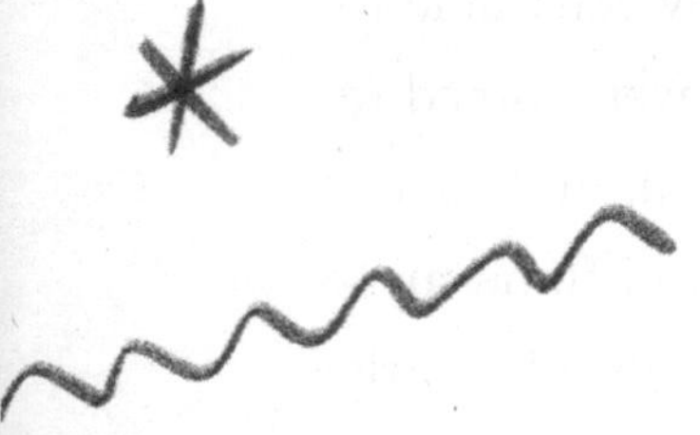

The nerd in the park

In my early twenties, I had a relationship end so badly that it sent me grey. I've had a few breakups over my slutty little life, all of them varying in severity and, for most of them, I was the one who had ended things. But this one was the kind where I could barely catch my breath from hurt, where the only time I felt relief was midway through crying. Basically what I'm saying is that this time I wasn't the one who had ended it. I had been dumped.

When people say that it's worse to break up with someone than be broken up with, I just laugh, baffled by how they can go around pretending to believe that. Being broken up with is absolutely the worst of the two, because the person you love is sitting across from you, essentially telling you that they're okay with never knowing you in the same way again. Plus there's all the time you spend standing at the sink, washing dishes and convincing yourself you'll never love again. Even if you were able to find it within yourself to try to meet someone new, who could be bothered when there's so much effort involved in building up intimacy with a total stranger? There are so many inane questions that have to be asked at the start of getting to know someone.

'So, do you have siblings?'

'No. I had a twin, but they died in the womb.'

Jesus.

'So … what countries have you been to?'

I hate that part. I just want to jump straight into the bit where they know how hard to choke me and promise they'll be there for me when my parents die.

During this time of deep breakup depression, one of my friends suggested a walk in the park to cheer me up, which was a big mistake, as most suburban parks depress me. I'm not sure what it is about them; I think it has something to do with when my parents would take me to parks after their divorce, and being aware as a child on these outings that my mum, who'd be chain-smoking cigarettes a few metres away from me, might not be having as much fun as I was. I also think it has something to do with resenting authority and not wanting to have a nice time in the place that the council has designated for that purpose. Or maybe it's because if you're feeling depressed, it's one of the things people suggest doing to make yourself feel better, which means the park is often just full of depressed people.

I went along on the walk anyway, because I'm good at sensing when sympathy and goodwill is drying up. My friends took me to a fairly isolated park and, as we were walking through the trees, we heard a blood-curdling scream coming from a distant corner. For a split second, I was worried that my friends had enlisted some kind of pagan organisation that put sad, moping women out of their misery. A second scream rang out and the severity of it filled me with dread, like I was hearing a person being murdered. We jogged over to where we suspected the screams had originated and what we saw was much worse than a murder. As we approached the clearing in the park, we discovered that it was four adults between the ages of twenty-five to fifty 'live action role playing' or, as they call it, LARPing.

If you don't know what LARPing is, it is when a group of people who are eligible to vote choose to dress up in costumes and interact with each other as characters from video games or fantasy novels. I know it sounds as though I'm putting it down, but I'm actually not. I'll admit, they look like they're having a lot of fun. Plus, who am I to judge? That very afternoon I had been caught taking selfies of myself whipping my head around to see what I looked like caught off-guard.

However, this particular group of nerdy adults were being particularly obnoxious, and, on closer inspection, it became clear that the screaming was emanating from one man in particular, who was writhing around on the ground dressed as a steampunk butterfly as another man pretended to spear him with a sword.

Why is it that being sexually rejected by women results in such loud hobbies for some men? It reminds me of my neighbour, who insists on revving his motorbike engine for five minutes in his driveway in a menacing pre-show, before accelerating loudly just as he reaches my house. It's so deafening I can barely hear the details of his divorce below the sound of his two-stroke.

For a while, there was this trend where girls would talk about how they liked 'nerdy guys' – yet, watching the scene before me, I'm pretty sure that if faced with the reality of being in a relationship with a true nerd, they'd change their tune. They don't really want a nerd; they want a hunk who wears glasses, can download movies and won't cheat on them with their best friend. If you really want a nerd, there they are, girls – in the park, wearing capes and chasing around their bald friend, who's pretending a broom is a horse and squealing at the top of his lungs.

I don't know what came over me in that moment, but I decided to walk over there and let them know that, while I didn't have a problem with their hobby, perhaps the screaming might be a bit much on a Saturday afternoon. I approached the man I assumed was the head nerd, as he was holding a big leatherbound book and barking orders at the others, and tapped him on the shoulder.

What I intended to say was, 'Hi, I don't want to be rude, but my friends and I were walking past and we heard really loud screaming and thought something terrible was happening, so maybe it's best to keep it down a bit.'

But all I got out was 'Hi—' before being immediately interrupted.

'Sorry, I have a girlfriend. I'm not interested,' he spat.

I was stunned. Not just because he had a girlfriend but because he was so sure I was approaching him for sex! The confidence he displayed almost made me want to have sex with him right then and there. It was very confusing. I ended up mumbling some sort of apology and slunk off back to my group of friends, feeling somehow less desirable than before.

I know I come off a little mean in that story, but at the time I remember having a revelatory thought: nerds can also be really mean.

There's this narrative in storytelling that the nerdy kid who gets bullied is always in the right and the bully is always in the wrong. I think it's unfair, because we all have the capacity to make each other feel bad. But it's the nerds who did their schoolwork who are better equipped with the tools they need to tell their story, when they emerge on the other side of schooling. So they go on to write books and movies where the mean bullies are defeated and the nerd is revealed to be the hero.

The bullies I encountered, however, were generally from families where the parents were horrible or absent and gave their kid no boundaries, and because of this the kid rarely attained a tertiary education and usually ended up in an undesirable job. They were typically, therefore, unable to defend themselves when the victims of their bullying painted them as villains, born cruel. Bullies rarely get to explain where they're coming from. If you had parents who treated you with neglect and forced you to grow up quickly, then it's no wonder why you'd get to school and be infuriated by the confidence of someone who had parents who packed their lunches perfectly every day and told them they were brilliant.

I grew up in a very low socio-economic area and I was friends with bullies. I was also bullied, sometimes by those very same friends. There was a girl called Sarah who I was good friends with for many years, though she really terrified me. My mum was always hesitant about letting me go to Sarah's house, because it smelt like cigarettes and had walls with holes in them where people had punched them in. Every time we were there, the house was full of adults who were clearly drunk and on drugs, but it didn't matter to us at the time; it just meant we could stay up late and drink cans of Coke and no one would say anything. I loved it.

Over the next few years, my friend transitioned into what could really only be described as my bully. She used to push me over into bushes and spread vicious rumours about me. I could never understand what it was about me that had pissed her off so much.

It wasn't just me copping the brunt though – she had it out for everyone, especially one girl who was a bit of a nerd. One day, the girl decided she'd had enough of Sarah's shit and announced at school that she was going to kill herself, then ran off in a big dramatic display. The teachers were freaking out because they had found an envelope in her locker that they'd assumed was a suicide note, but they couldn't be sure because no one could read Elvish (a fictionalised language from *The Lord of the Rings*). In order to locate her, the teachers had to find a kid with the credentials to decipher this note, and become bullies themselves to get that kid to translate it. They immediately singled out a boy in the year below, because his name was Lorkin and he had bacne, and they were right, he *was* fluent in Elvish. After some cajoling and a few threats, the boy duly told them where the note said she'd be.

After they found her, I remember the way my drama teacher, Mrs McCarthy, who was openly drunk during school hours, announced it to us. 'She's been found at the back of the oval,' she slurred, matter-of-factly.

We all gasped and asked if she was okay.

Mrs McCarthy snapped, 'Oh, she's fine. She'd taken four Panadols; she probably felt better.' Then she knocked back another swig of whiskey from her coffee cup.

The girl who was bullied by Sarah is now thriving, by the way. The last I heard of her, she was engaged and working as a tour guide operator in the Whitsundays.

Months after the incident in the park, I was back in Brisbane telling an old friend about the nerd who had belittled and sexually rejected me, and how shocked I had been at my deep desire to bully him.

She said that, funnily enough, she'd run into our school bully/friend Sarah at a shopping centre a few weeks earlier. They'd sat down for a coffee and caught up on the past eight years or so, which had turned out to be pretty full on for Sarah. She was now a mum and had been dealing with severe drug and alcohol problems for a number of years.

Meanwhile, the only thing my friend was suffering from was a huge bout of middle-class guilt, as she revealed to Sarah that she'd lived in Paris for a couple of years and dropped out of multiple university degrees.

As they were getting ready to wrap things up, Sarah had apparently gone a bit quiet and then asked my friend if she could tell her something. She went on to explain that her drug and alcohol problems had stemmed from the fact that, at age thirteen, unbeknownst to us all, her mum had been letting her stepdad's friends have sex with her in exchange for drugs and money. She said that she's always felt bad about how much of a bitch she was to everyone at school, and that whenever she gets the opportunity to apologise, she does.

When I heard this, just like that, the things Sarah had said to me during school didn't seem so bad. Of course she had bullied us – she had every right to be irrationally angry. Yet, for many people in our year, including myself up until that moment, she'd been immortalised as simply a bad person who had got what she deserved in life.

It's a symptom of binary storytelling in movies and TV where the bullies are bad and the kids they bully are good and deserve justice that we tend to make those same assumptions about people. But life is much more complicated than that. And I'm not trying to downplay the devastating effect bullying can have on people. For so many people like myself, being bullied by a kid at high school will remain one of the greatest injustices they will ever suffer in life. It's not fair to be bullied.

But it's a privilege to come from a home where things are fair.

For me, my fear of Sarah was not just about what she would do or say to me, but how completely unfazed she was by the consequences she might face. It turned out Sarah had been completely unfazed because the worst punishment anyone could give her was nothing compared to what was happening at home.

So thank you, nerd in the park – your actions got me thinking more about how we think of bullies and, in the process, I was able to forgive Sarah and understand what motivated her all those years ago. I now look back on that time and think how lucky I am that I didn't have a reason to be a bully myself.

The woman in the castle

A few years ago, I received a terse phone call from my dad. He informed me that my stepmum had been involved in an accident.

When I asked him what had happened, he began clearing his throat over and over again. After a few attempts at getting the story out of him while he steadfastly avoided my questions, I just began naming potentially affected body parts. 'Head? Stomach? Her leg? Her foot?'

There was a long silence. 'Ahh, a bit higher than her foot,' he replied.

Eventually he came out with the whole story. She'd gone on a ride on their neighbour's new scooter in her Peter Alexander pyjamas, fallen off, and in the process had somehow managed to vaginally impale herself. I imagine it was on the kickstand, or perhaps even the handlebar – I've never asked what it was on exactly, because I don't really want the answer. As ridiculous as the incident sounded, it was a serious accident that required her to go to hospital so they could make sure there hadn't been any internal damage. A truly suburban nightmare.

My stepmum never wanted to discuss her scooter accident, which was fair enough. That is, until one night after she'd downed four margaritas, and clearly decided to try to own the narrative.

It's my belief that everyone, given the right stimulants, can perform, and this was her night. She got up and began strutting around the living room, regaling me and four family friends with a fairly sanitised version of events. Then, sensing she needed a strong closer, she ended the story with, 'So yes, basically I fucked a scooter!'

It was a shocking finale. My fairly conservative stepmum, who had been quite proud of the fact that in her whole life she'd only slept with two men, had now publicly revealed her third conquest.

I'd like to mention that this whole scooter incident happened only months before the holiday where my dad jumped into a pool without checking underwater and split his ball sack wide open, requiring twelve stitches. Interestingly, I didn't have to pry much that time to get the information out of him.

'Split my sack open!' he sang out over the phone.

These two incidents also occurred in the same year my stepmum was attacked by a bat in the middle of Brisbane city in broad daylight.

This series of cursed events is important to keep in mind as I detour a little bit to tell you about the woman to whom the scooter belonged.

I had always been fascinated by this woman with long, black, shiny hair who lived near my dad and stepmum out in the suburbs, in a gothic-style house that looked like a castle and dwarfed all the other houses nearby. The life of the woman who lived there looked so traditionally perfect that I knew it couldn't possibly be the case – but, then again, maybe it was. She and her husband had two cute kids, aged one and five, and two matching BMWs that sat side by side in their tidy garage. She'd smile easily to all the neighbours.

As I was walking past one day, she called me over and asked if I'd be interested in doing some nannying for her. I was eighteen, needed the money and was desperate to get a look inside the house, so I agreed.

'Wonderful, darling. Come over tomorrow morning,' she said.

The next day, I rang the doorbell a few times. No one answered, so I walked around the back and found her drunk and completely naked with her two kids, splashing around in the pool. It occurred to me in that moment, as I stared at both of her nipples, that I didn't actually know her name.

My first job that day was to order a bucket of KFC and run her a hot bath, while also preparing lunch for the kids, during which time she poured herself several more glasses of wine. I made sure to heap the bath with soap so there would be lots of bubbles to cover her enormous breasts (which were an anniversary gift from her husband, she later told me). After the kids had eaten and I'd successfully put them both down for a nap, she put on a luxurious robe, took me by the hand and walked me through the house, showing me all of her wonderful things and recounting stories of her youth. She unapologetically told me about her desire from age sixteen to find a rich man, and how this had led to years of coke-fuelled parties on yachts, and spending her twenties dating sixty-year-old finance men who still ended up leaving her for someone even younger. The whole thing just felt so clichéd to me. If you wrote her as a character in a script, you'd be told she lacked depth and believability.

She despondently toyed with her crystal glassware and then brightly declared that I should come upstairs and go through her wardrobe with her. We were upstairs for barely a minute before she burst into tears, and then broke into a watery smile and insisted that I have her diamond necklace and fur coat.

This would happen like clockwork each time I went over: she'd drink, take me upstairs and, with her wild, drunken eyes boring into mine, she'd push her luxurious items into my hands. It was sort of understood that I'd politely accept them, then return them all the next morning, when she'd be waiting sheepishly at the door, ready to take them from my arms, while whispering urgent apologies about her behaviour the previous day.

I understood that her desire to give me her things came from a need to feel close to someone, and it made me sad when I realised that this must be how a lot of rich people tried to form intimacy. Didn't she realise we could just bitch about someone we both knew?

She had a kind heart, but she was so relentlessly stupid and I came to resent her for how powerless she was. One glass of wine in, she'd brag about how she'd successfully bagged a rich man, then four glasses in, she'd curl up into a ball and tell me she had nothing of her own and couldn't even use a computer.

'Darling, I can't even type. I never had to.' She couldn't help but boast even when she was trying to feel sorry for herself.

Her husband was a puny man with wispy blond hair and zero chin, who, instead of being a decent person and providing his kids with any love or guidance whatsoever, made the choice to be a massive arsehole instead. One of my jobs at the end of the day was to vacuum all the dirt and dust off the ground. To make sure I'd done the job properly, when he got home he'd take his socks off and walk around to check there was nothing underfoot. One night I had run out of time between making dinner and putting the kids to sleep, so I'd not been able to get to the vacuuming. He stood there, barefoot, in a three-piece suit, screaming at the top of his lungs over and over again, 'There's dirt under my feet!'

He was a caricature of a bad husband, a man who I felt was incapable of showing genuine affection. He spoke to his wife like she was a work-experience kid on her first day at the office, getting everything wrong and messing up coffee orders. There was no respect or tenderness in his tone of voice, and there would be a collective household shudder when we heard his car pull up at night.

I always found it strange that he couldn't even *pretend* to be a loving man in the presence of me, an outsider. If he was happy to act like this in front of me, I couldn't bear to think what life with him was like behind closed doors.

In 2017, my family was on some fabulous holiday overseas and I was at home in Sydney, toying with the idea of taking a weed edible given to me by a comedian from the US. He had explicitly warned me I should only take half at most. The thing was, I had nothing on all day, so I didn't see the harm in taking all of it – my nature has always been to do more of something to ensure I don't end up with half the experience.

I ate the whole thing before lunchtime and felt it almost immediately, a warm numbing sensation crashing through my extremities, and I knew immediately that I should have listened to him. By 3 pm, I could barely move, yet my mind was racing a million miles an hour. Complete paranoia took over me. I began sending strange messages to past boyfriends, explaining how they'd 'never really been there for me', then listening to Blink-182 songs before bursting into tears at the thought of my mum making dinner for herself.

Around 5 pm, I gave in to the heavy sensation weighing down on me and fell into a deep sleep, feeling like I'd never wake up. I did wake up, though, around 10 pm. I looked at my phone and among the confused messages from people I hadn't talked to in years were four missed calls from the woman in the gothic-style castle house. I remembered that my stepmum had told me if I needed to get into their house or wanted to get in contact with them, she'd given their holiday information and keys to the woman up the street. 'You know, the one you used to babysit for?'

I sat upright. I hadn't talked to her properly for seven years. What did she want from me? Then I remembered my accident-prone family and my residual paranoia got me thinking that this woman might be trying to contact me to tell me they had all died in some horrific turn of events. My heart was beating so fast I could barely use my fingers to call her back. When I eventually did, she picked up on the second ring.

'Darling?' she said, her voice dripping with concern.

My eyes welled up. I couldn't believe this was how I was going to find out my dad had died: stoned out of my mind, fingers covered in hours-old Cheezels dust.

'Darling, I have something to tell you,' she went on. 'As you know your family are overseas, and ...'

I held the phone away from my body while a silent sob erupted from me.

'Darling? Darling?' I could hear her repeat.

I bravely put the phone back to my ear.

'Yes?' I said, just wanting it to be over.

'Darling … I didn't have anyone else to call but I've finally done it. I'm leaving him.'

She was leaving her husband. She'd called me after seven years to tell me about her divorce.

'Fucking hell!' I exclaimed. Before she could respond, I hung up on her and fell back onto my bed.

It wasn't her fault I was stoned and thought the worst, but I didn't care. I was just so happy my clumsy family was alive.

So thank you to the woman in the big castle house for the harsh lesson that if someone tells you to take half of something, then just take half. They're trying to help you.

My very poor sex education

I'm quite sexually repressed, broadly speaking. I haven't always been, but I'm finding as I get older the whole concept of sex seems like too much bother.

I suppose a more accurate description of my feelings towards sex these days is that I'm not on the lookout to broaden my sexual horizon, and I often get sick of the idea that we have to push the boundaries every time we do it. I'm happy to admit and even commit to the page that I *like* the missionary position. I get sick of people bemoaning missionary and equating it to the flavour vanilla, which I also happen to think is pretty great. They are two equally great things that I can enjoy any night of the week.

People always want to put down the things that are most popular, but vanilla has earned its spot at the top for a reason. It has classic appeal, it works well with other flavours, it doesn't overpower the senses, and it doesn't show off. People will always need vanilla as an option on days when mint choc chip or passionfruit swirl are too much.

And similarly, to bring it back to the missionary position, you can't deny that without being able to come back to one of the classics, none of the other stuff would seem very exciting at all.

My first introduction to sex was during a backyard family gathering one sunny afternoon, when my three-year-old sister slithered up the fence and began rubbing herself up against the pool gate. This wasn't the first time she'd done this; in fact, randomly humping things had sort of become her thing. My stepmum's sister pointed it out with barely concealed shock and my stepmum, who was three gins to the wind at that point, told her to relax, ignore it, and just let her finish.

My stepmum's reaction was uncommon. In my experience, most adults tended to freak out when they saw us kids displaying sexual behaviour, which I totally understand now, but we couldn't understand what it was we were doing wrong. When I was in kindergarten, a boy named Zac approached me and asked if I'd like to see his penis and in return would it be okay if I showed him my vagina. It seemed like a pretty standard transaction, so I agreed, and we disappeared underneath the playground equipment where he pulled down his shorts and showed me his, quite frankly, tiny penis. I looked at it for a bit and then, remembering my part of the deal, dutifully lifted up my skirt to show him what I was working with, which was when the teacher found us. She immediately put me in timeout, and through the shutters, I watched, absolutely furious, as Zac continued to laugh and play with the other children on the slide and in the tyre tunnel.

Funnily enough, despite most adults' discomfort when it comes to children and their sexual discoveries, parents are supposed to be the ones to teach you about sex. But when my friends and I try to recall what lessons we were taught about sex by our parents, it's clear that none of them really figured out how best to do this. I have sympathy for parents who are supposed to carry out this monumental task – how exactly do you teach kids about something like sex? It reminds me of the time somebody asked me how I would describe the internet to a person in the 1500s. I didn't know where to begin. It's very hard to articulate something that is so complicated and hard to summarise – it's just there, we're all supposed to do it and it's pretty good.

My boyfriend recalls his dad driving him to school at age ten and telling him that soon he was going to experience a pleasant sensation followed by a substance coming out of his penis. This abstract explanation left my boyfriend, whose pleasure still came mainly from the exchanging of Pokemon cards, thoroughly confused. A couple of weeks later, again while driving to school, his dad said that he'd talked to some of the men at work about their conversation and they'd all agreed that actually that advice was probably a couple of years too early.

'Just forget I said anything,' his dad said awkwardly, and after that he never mentioned anything to do with sex again.

This seems to be a common thread I've stumbled across. Parents, perhaps wanting to get the sex talk out of the way before they receive the withering stare of a fully fledged teenager, give too much information too soon. I remember being not even twelve and my mum telling me that sex feels better once the man has made the woman orgasm. It felt to me that instead of being given 'the sex talk', I was being told something that more resembled sex tips and tricks. I'm surprised she didn't wink and tell me that sex actually feels better without a condom.

The closest my dad got to giving me the sex talk was the day he was driving me home from school and the song 'My Neck, My Back (Lick It)' by Khia came on the radio. We both sat next to each other in uncomfortable silence, my dad's knuckles white on the steering wheel, until he snapped and changed stations. He loudly declared that Beethoven would be spinning in his grave – a statement that was as cringeworthy to me as the experience we'd just been through together.

When it came to sex, having been told almost nothing of value by our parents, it's no wonder we were left to piece together what we could from movies, TV shows and out-of-context conversations. But this obviously left quite a few gaps in our knowledge.

When my mum went away on tour and decided to leave me at home, I would often stay with a Czechoslovakian woman named Adrianna, who had a daughter my age also called Adrianna, and a son, Tomas, who was a bit younger. The first time I met her daughter, she arrived with her mother at our house and we shyly introduced ourselves. After my mum and and the older Adrianna spoke for a while, the daughter asked her mum when she was going to get her surprise.

'This is your surprise: me introducing you to your new friend. She's going to come and stay with us for a few weeks,' her mother replied.

The daughter burst into tears and had a full five-minute breakdown while I watched on, sympathetic but slightly put out. I still don't like it when I'm with a friend on my way to a party or gathering and they call the host and say, 'And you'll never guess who I'm bringing!' or words to that effect. Why even give the person a chance to get excited only to be disappointed by my presence? Better to not say anything at all and if they're happy to see me, that's their own business.

In conjunction with the Adriannas' general cynicism and casual depression, which most Slavic or Eastern European people seem to have, Adrianna's husband/dad had just recently taken off back to his country that didn't exist anymore, which did nothing to help improve their moods. Despite this, I loved staying with their family and, having Russian family of my own, their dispositions suited me just fine. Adrianna and I became fast friends and over the years we spent thousands of hours in each other's company, playing as many games as we could.

Like most kids, we were vaguely familiar with the concept of sex, so one of our favourite games was 'having sex', where Adrianna and I would take our clothes off, get under the doona cover and just lie there together. As both our parents were divorced, the game would then include a fiery argument where we'd both agree that 'it wasn't working'. Then we would 'break up' and have a discussion about who was going to take the kids on what weekend.

In fact, the clearest sexual education I ever received came from my friend Sophie. In Year Nine, she told me that she'd been making herself orgasm with her hand. She said that she'd been able to have orgasms ever since she was much younger and would mount the pool cleaner as it jigged along doing its thing. That made me think of my little sister and the pool gate, and I started to wonder whether I was the only one in the world who'd had a platonic relationship with the pool.

That night, I went to bed and, following Sophie's instructions, tried to have an orgasm of my own. While it all felt quite good, it wasn't really anything to go on about the way Sophie had. The next day, I told this to Sophie. She said that I hadn't actually had one and when I did, I would know. She said I just had to push through and keep going and that eventually it would work.

For the next couple of nights, I came close to something, but I knew it wasn't it. Then one night I felt I was onto a good thing and then it kept getting better and better and then it happened, and I finally understood what she meant when she said that I'd know.

To be perfectly honest, I'm glad I didn't have parents who taught me about sex in a normal and healthy way. I quite like the old-fashioned way of figuring it out for yourself with the help of fellow misinformed friends. I know that correct parenting these days probably means uncomfortable yet informative conversations that lead to young people being equipped with a healthy view of sex, but I think I prefer the shameful secretive way that I found out about it all. There have to be some things that continue to carry shame; it's a tradition. Plus shame can be good as a backup for when guilt isn't enough. Because, let me tell you, once I learnt how to make myself orgasm, I was an animal. Sure, I felt guilty for how many times I would do it in a day, sometimes running off to the bathrooms during school to do it. But it was shame that stopped me from rubbing myself up against the pool gate.

So thank you to my poor sex education for providing me with the opportunity to figure out my own personal journey, which has ultimately led me to my boring, safe, Nicole Kidman-esque sexuality.

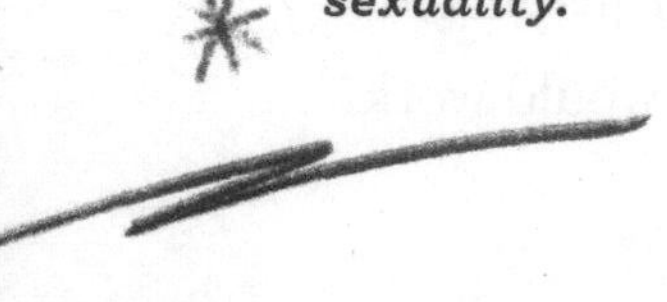

The worst gigs of my life: part one

When you start out in comedy, you're pretty desperate for two things: stage time and money. And in those early days, if there's the promise of both, it's incredible what gigs you'll say yes to. Which is how I ended up saying yes to performing at a Mexican food franchise in the middle of the day to promote their new three-dollar taco meal.

This sort of thing gets offered to comedians all the time. Someone who works in events or PR will go to a great night of comedy and marvel at how it all seems so off-the-cuff and easy. Then, after about three beers or so, they'll think, why not use this to promote their product?

The truth is that good comedy happens in places where someone has put a lot of thought into the sound, the lighting, the way people are seated and the ease at which you can get a drink, and if all of those things are just right, then maybe, just maybe, it works.

The exact pitch for this gig was that this particular chain wanted to get a different comedian to perform at every store on the same day all across Australia. They figured these impromptu shows would be an uproarious success and that the randomness of it was sure to go viral.

This sounded like a terrible idea to everyone who was asked to do it, but the fee was five hundred dollars and a free meal, so nearly every comedian they approached said yes. The problem was that there were simply not enough professional comedians to have one at each of their stores Australia-wide, so, in the end, most of the people who ended up doing it were very new to comedy, including myself.

Most comedians got to perform in their local restaurant, or at least one relatively close by, so it wasn't that big of a deal if it didn't go well – they could simply eat their free meal and slink out afterwards, five hundred dollars richer. But, for some reason, I was asked to perform at a store in a town in regional Queensland. I was to be flown two and a half hours north to do ten minutes of stand-up comedy to a bunch of unsuspecting customers who were just there to wolf down a secret burrito in their lunch break.

I boarded the plane, not knowing what I was in for but thinking that as long as there were four walls, a microphone and a speaker, it couldn't be too bad. Once I landed, I turned on my phone and was bombarded with texts from my comedian friends, who regaled me with horror stories from their gigs thus far. Some had turned up to stores where the staff had no idea what was happening, and there was no microphone or space for them to perform. Luckily, most of those who encountered this scenario were turned away and told they would still get paid, which is the ideal outcome.

Others had performed anyway and been mercilessly bullied by passers-by. One of my friends did the gig at one of the franchises situated in an outdoor mall. He told me there were kids on bikes doing laps around him, calling him a 'fuckin' poof'. At one point, he thought they'd gone for good, but they had just left to rally more of the troops and returned with ten or so more kids who had some of their own customised insults ready to go.

These stories filled me with dread, but also some hope that maybe I would also be turned away – that way I could fly home and still pocket the money without having to humiliate myself.

I waited in the pick-up area for the franchisee, who was going to drive me to and from the airport as had been arranged by the promoters. After waiting a while, I eventually heard four vicious beeps that came from a silver Toyota Camry.

'G'day, I'm Trudi! Get in!' barked the driver, a woman in her mid-fifties with a face painted like a tiger.

I got in the car and it became clear that I would not be as lucky as some of the others. In fact, Trudi couldn't wait to tell me that her store was extremely prepared for today and very excited to have a comedian come and perform!

'We had a big staff meeting about it last night,' she said excitedly, as I began experiencing the early stages of a panic attack. 'We can't wait to see the comedy. We've put up balloons, we've got a face painter,' she jabbered on, pointing at her face like I might have thought that was her regular day look.

I tried to match her enthusiasm by asking questions. 'So when we get to the restaurant, what—'

She held a hand up to stop me. 'Oh, it's not a restaurant, darl. We're in the food court in a shopping centre.'

My heart sank.

'We've put everything into the place. It's been a struggle, but we're finally starting to see some returns. Mexican food is only getting more and more popular. But my husband's a cunt – you'll see, biggest cunt you'll ever meet.'

As much as I had been dreading the gig, I had at least envisaged doing the show at an actual restaurant with a little stage area and a good sound system. But when we arrived, I realised she wasn't lying – it was literally in a food court, sandwiched between a Terry White chemist and a McDonald's.

I tried to keep calm and look as though I was a professional, but inside I was a nervous wreck. Trudi didn't pick up on my energy at all and instead began eagerly introducing me to the employees: a couple of pimply teens and an older Korean woman who looked very uncomfortable with having to have her face painted.

I briefly thought about getting my face painted too. *How good is the artist?* I wondered. *Can he make me look like a completely different person? Perhaps I can convince people that I'm Carl Barron?*

I wanted to throw myself in front of a car so I wouldn't have to perform. Instead I was plonked down at a plastic table and chairs in the food court and handed a chicken burrito, which I choked down while going over my very limited material, trying to figure out what set could possibly work here, considering my act at the time centred mostly around my vagina and the men who'd been inside it. I looked around – the only other people in the almost-deserted food court were some tradies in hi-vis singlets looking at their phones, a couple of ratbags who looked like they should have been at the magistrates court rather than the food court, and a woman and her child who were sitting in stony-faced silence eating their McDonald's Happy Meals. None of these people looked like they were up for an impromptu comedy show. You show me someone on their lunch break who wants to make eye contact with anyone, let alone an inexperienced comedian like myself.

I continued to spiral. Every now and then I'd look up from my table and Trudi would be watching me, her gleeful face beaming like crazy over the glass countertop. Each time we made eye contact, she'd give me the double thumbs-up. I'd meekly return the thumbs up, arrange my face into the best version of a smile I could muster, and then keep obsessively scrolling my phone, as news of my friends' cancelled gigs continued to roll in.

Eventually Trudi's cunt husband came over to me, wheeling a little portable speaker with a microphone attached, like the ones used by people who spruik products outside of men's clothing stores that cater to fellows on the larger side.

'That's my microphone, is it?' I laughed as he brought it over.

'Yeah, is that gonna work for you?' he replied with not even a hint of a smile. I could tell that it was going to have to work for me.

'Trudi reckons you should start in the next five minutes,' he said, then he walked away. I sat next to my little speaker with an attached microphone, feeling like I was about to be taken to the gallows.

The actual 'performance' is a bit of blur – my brain simply won't allow me to access the exact memory of what happened lest it send me to a loony bin. But here's what I remember: I stood up with resolve and wheeled the speaker through the table and chairs, trying not to knock into anyone. I eventually ended up in a spot halfway between the counter of the Mexican place and where the food court seating began. I timidly began the official spiel about the new taco meal that I'd been given by the promoters, and then explained that what was happening here was happening nationwide and there was a hashtag people could use if they wanted to 'tweet about it'. I saw an elderly woman shaking her head as she packed up her handbag and walked away, and who could blame her – her husband had probably died in a war for my freedom to do this.

I then awkwardly launched into the first minute of my stand-up routine, which you could barely hear over the din of the shopping centre music. At first, there were a few middle-aged people who smiled at me encouragingly, but once I told my first dirty joke, all goodwill was lost. The mother put her hands over her child's ears and they walked away. She turned back for a moment to give me a look that was far dirtier than my joke.

I looked away from her and locked eyes with a fifty-something-year-old man who had joined the chorus of people forlornly shaking their heads at me. He kept clutching at his wife's arm, as though checking to make sure his idea of what a woman should be was still real. I tried to keep going, but the microphone was crackling in and out, and people kept standing up to leave or, worse, chatting among themselves, obviously bored by my anguish.

I thought about Jesus receiving his lashes in public. It must have gone on for some time, and surely after the first horrific fifteen minutes, people started to get bored and left. Not that I'm comparing myself to Jesus, but if you're suffering in public, you at least want people to be interested in it. It's somehow worse for them to be bored by it.

It was one of the most humiliating moments of my life, made even worse by the fact that after two minutes or so, Trudi came over to me and said, 'That's okay, love, that's enough. It's not working.'

I agreed with her, thanked the non-existent crowd, then clipped the microphone back onto the speaker and wheeled it over to my plastic seat.

'I'll just finish up with this burrito order and I'll whizz you back to the airport, alright, love?' said Trudi.

I thought the trip *to* the gig was bad, but it was nothing compared to the trip back. I had to sit there knowing I'd disappointed an entire workplace, and the hardest thing was that Trudi's face was still painted like a tiger. We drove mostly in silence, except for the few times she recommended I check out various comedians she'd seen over the years who were really funny.

'You know, we get all the big comics here, and they're great. It's just practice, isn't it, love? You just need a few more years under your belt,' she said, smiling at me sympathetically.

I nodded wearily, wondering how those comedians she'd listed would go performing in a shopping-centre food court.

To her credit, though, she wasn't wrong. A couple more years was all I needed and I would never have to do a gig like that again. Or so I thought.

The worst gigs of my life: part two

Some years after the Mexican food franchise fiasco, my manager asked me if I wanted to do a couple of regional gigs over the course of a week or so, starting in Longreach, Queensland, for an initiative being run by the local council. I said yes, because the money was good and, like all things I say yes to that I end up regretting, I reasoned that it couldn't possibly be that bad.

The gigs were a comedy competition, which was supposed to be a way of getting the community involved in the performing arts. The way it worked was that each night we'd travel to different towns where anyone could get up and do five minutes of stand-up comedy, then Luke Heggie, another comedian friend, and I would decide who was best on the night and they'd be invited to compete in the grand final. After the competition bit of the night, Luke and I were then required to perform twenty minutes of our own acts. Though I was nervous about performing for a mainly older, conservative crowd who'd grown up on cattle country for the majority of their lives, I thought it could be a good chance to get away. It was only when I was handed a box of Vegemite, which was to be the prize for the winner, that I realised what I might be in for.

When we arrived in Longreach, we were picked up by a disgruntled council worker called Kevin, who, upon meeting us, started bemoaning the fact that he couldn't get any comedians 'from the television' so he ended up having to book us. In complete silence, he drove us to the place where we would be performing on the first night, already angry at us for being, in his mind, not up to the task. The venue was essentially a large shed masquerading as an RSL, but really it just seemed like a place where people could bash each other undercover if the rums didn't sit well with them.

There was a woman in thongs who managed the bar. She could have been anywhere between twenty or ninety-eight years old – with her diet of beef and Winfield Blues, it was pretty hard to tell. She showed us the performance area they'd set up for us, which was complete with a tinny microphone that didn't so much amplify our voices as warp them so we sounded as nasal as the locals did.

The only entrant on the first night of the competition was a woman called Big Jules, who for some reason lunged at me as soon as we walked into the building, then apologised immediately. She then began lurching around and bobbing her head up and down, while screaming at her beer. Then she stopped, looked at the bar fridge and called it a cunt.

Everyone seemed to know her and, as most small communities do, they'd accepted her as one of their own and treated her with more care and consideration than you would ever see in a more urban area, which tend to be populated with culturally bereft inner-city professionals who share posts online about the need to de-stigmatise mental health while calling the cops on homeless people.

Big Jules got on stage, wearing speed-dealer sunglasses and her hat to the side. Her 'routine' consisted of her muttering some incomprehensible nonsense into the microphone. This got a few people more confident, and a big man called Cocky took to the stage and told a joke-book joke, which absolutely destroyed.

It was then my turn as the so-called professional comedian to get up and show them how it was done. Unfortunately, country people have limited tolerance for jokes about what it's like being a single girl living in a city that provides literally every creature comfort you could ever want. It was made clear to me early on in my set that I was neither likeable nor relatable, and a table of middle-aged women made sure I knew how they felt. After every joke, they would roll their eyes, take big sips of their white wines, and then one of them would say something snide to the others, which would set them off into giggling fits. I could at least say that I made them laugh through the act of bonding together in their hatred of me and, to be honest, sometimes that's all you can do. I've often finished a show by claiming that even if you hated what I did, at least I've provided you some fodder for discussion in the car ride home.

After struggling through my time, it was Luke's turn. As he delivered his first punchline, someone struck it big on one of the pokie machines, and the sound of coins falling into the metal tray reverberated throughout the otherwise silent room. Kevin just watched on with his head in his hands.

After finishing up the show and declaring Cocky with his joke-book joke the winner, we bashfully packed up. Kevin dropped us at our motel, where he informed us that there would be a tour manager called Lorenzo coming to meet us, and Lorenzo would be driving us to the more regional gigs over the next week.

Lorenzo arrived the next morning, wearing diamante-encrusted sunglasses and a gold chain necklace. He proclaimed himself to be a traditional European boy who was a wedding DJ, owned his own photo-booth hire company and had just recently moved out of home at the ripe age of thirty-four. I knew then that we were in for a week of gritted teeth and derisive comments said under our breaths.

He couldn't have encountered two people who were less up for wanting to get to know him. Luke is a no-nonsense married dad of two and I was in one of my more depressive states, and this, combined with the sinking realisation of what we'd signed up for, meant that neither of us were up for any of the conversation Lorenzo slung our way.

That didn't stop Lorenzo from trying though. After hours of driving in silence, both Luke and I preferring to keep our eyes on the desert road rather than engage with him, Lorenzo piped up about how good of a DJ he was. Then he ran us through all of his Spotify playlists and insisted we follow them. We both declined in unison. Unfazed, he barrelled ahead, telling us that his favourite song was 'Smooth' by Santana featuring Rob Thomas.

Perhaps the most annoying thing about Lorenzo was that, no matter what you said to him to attempt to break his spirit, he never let it get to him. His ego and self-esteem were seemingly made of steel, impervious to the flames I kept trying to light. Luke and I would try to sneak off for breakfast in the mornings, but Lorenzo would always find us. I eventually gave him the nickname 'Weed' and when he asked why, I told him it was because he kept popping up in places he wasn't wanted. He thought this was hilarious and referred to himself as Weed for the rest of the trip.

Luke and I performed in different towns every night, never to more than fourteen people. As the days wore on, and we had to endure long car rides with Lorenzo, I began thinking more and more about opening the car door and jumping out.

One trip, Lorenzo interrupted my suicidal ideations. 'Do you think you'll talk about these shows in your act when you get home?' he asked.

I shrugged in a noncommittal way and continued staring out the car window, knowing full well that I was definitely going to talk about *him* in my act.

There is no reason I should receive the amount of praise I do simply for standing up onstage and insisting that people listen to me. So thank you to the worst gigs of my life for forever keeping me humble.

Brett Jackson

In primary school, my friend Sophie and I did everything together. She was the perfect ally. We lived just up the road from each other, which was ideal for meeting up to play. It was also ideal when we fought, as it was just a five-minute walk home. We both played in the school band with flutes we'd hired, and we were both so bad at it that one time, just before a competition against a much better school, the music teacher told us that it would be best for everyone if we just mimed playing our instruments.

One of our more famous fights happened at the local fish-and-chip shop where we'd both decided to busk with our flutes at age ten. We wore Santa hats, even though it was April, and set up a little box into which people could toss their coins. At first, we were a hit. Looking back, I suppose it's because we were cute kids playing flutes adorably badly, and, come to think of it, people probably thought we had acute mental disorders because of the Santa hats. But we didn't feel cute, or mental – we felt like we were important businesswomen on the cusp of making some real money.

Things were going smoothly until Sophie wanted to play 'Home on the Range', which I didn't want to play, as I didn't feel it suited the vibe and clientele. This turned into a vicious fight with each of us saying such terrible things to the other that a woman dragged her child away from where we were playing (something that would become a recurring theme in my career). Fed up with it all, I decided to take my sheet music, flute and hat across the road and go it on my own. This made perfect sense; we clearly couldn't work together. It wasn't personal, it was just business. But to onlookers, all they saw were two ten-year-olds standing on either side of a busy main road wearing Santa hats, playing flutes badly and death-staring each other.

Now, the problem with allies is that they're only your ally until you both want the same thing, which Sophie and I often did. Then they become your competitor, and everyone knows that the more you know about your enemy, the fiercer the battle is.

One of our fiercest battles was over Brett Jackson. He was the cutest boy in Year Six and Sophie and I both had a crush on him. The selection of boys at our school left a lot to be desired, but Brett had just moved from Canada and had feminine features, nice teeth and a blonde bowl cut.

After school, we would sit on the floor of Sophie's bedroom and obsess over Brett's perfect bone structure, passionately explaining just what we'd do for a strand of his hair. We even performed witch spells together, in efforts to make ourselves irresistible to him.

He was always toying with our emotions, hinting at wanting to go out with one of us but not knowing which one to choose. We diligently worked as a team, trying to gather clues from his friends as to who he liked more, but it was all very coy and, also, we were all, like, eleven. It really seemed like, if anything was going to happen for either Sophie or me, it was going to be because of timing, and this meant any time we could get alone with him was precious.

Luckily, he was a bad boy who was constantly in trouble with his teachers and our exhausted principal. What this meant for us was that if we could sniff out where he'd been told to sit for half an hour as punishment, we could ask to go to the toilet and steal thirty seconds of alone-time with him.

One day, Brett had been caught lighting things on fire and I was told (by a boy who would go on to be on Australia's most-wanted list, though that's neither here nor there) that Brett had been sent to the principal's office to await punishment. The principal's office was at the end of a long covered concrete path, at the start of which were three concrete steps that had a bar above them, which was part of the support frame that held up the roof. It was customary, if you were heading down the stairs, to jump from the top step, grab hold of the overhead bar like you would on the monkey bars, and swing once, then land past the bottom step and continue walking.

As I walked past Brett outside the principal's office, praying he'd call out to me, he did, and my heart just burst. I sauntered over to him, feeling truly alive.

He spoke first. 'Becky? Can I ask you something?'

'Yeah …' I answered, imagining how I was going to break the news of our relationship to Sophie.

'Will you ask Sophie out for me?'

My eyes immediately filled with tears or, as I like to call them sometimes, liquid cool. My throat had closed up by this point, so I just sort of made a noise that sounded like a yes and walked down the path towards the stairs. If I didn't do the jump, I thought, he'd know beyond a doubt that I was upset, and I didn't want him to know. For some reason, I felt I had to prove to him that I was totally unaffected by him.

So I went for the jump.

Unfortunately, my hands were so slippery from the rejection sweat that, when I was supposed to swing back and then thrust my body forward to complete the landing, I instead lost my grip and fell back hard onto the concrete, breaking both my arms.

Not wanting him to know just how badly I was hurt, I stood up with both arms akimbo, laughed, told him I was fine, then immediately took myself to sick bay. Once there, the sadistic woman who ran that operation gave me two ice bags to put on each arm, then left the room. This was a major problem because the issue was that both my arms were broken, and I sort of needed my arms in order to hold the bags of ice against my arms properly. She swanned in half an hour later and diagnosed me as having two possibly sprained wrists, then sent me back to class where I gave the news about Brett to Sophie and saw out the last two hours of school in agonising pain. Plus my arms really hurt.

Sophie and Brett began dating the very next day, and I returned to school with both of my arms encased in plaster in a permanent double fist-pump. Not only did I miss out on the boy of my dreams but, to add insult to injury, I also needed help going to the toilet. Despite her winning our romantic competition, Sophie was above all else a loyal friend, and she would accompany me to the bathroom to help zip my culottes back up. As she did, she would tell me all about her new relationship with Brett and, thanks to the position of my plastered arms, I always looked as though I was really psyched for her.

Sophie and Brett broke up about a month later due to a misunderstanding about a Beanie Baby. It was rumoured that, during class, he'd gone through her locker and stolen one from her bag. He claimed that she'd said he could have it, and she said that was a bald-faced lie and that she'd merely mentioned the possibility of her lending it to him one day. Sophie and I both got over him together and set our sights on a new boy who'd arrived at school called Steven, who was far more mature and had hair that spiked upwards, a style that was now more popular than the bowl cut

By then, my arms had healed and I was able to resume my regular activities, including going to band practice, much to the chagrin of my music teacher, who had been hoping I'd never be able to play the flute again.

Thank you to Brett Jackson for the vital lesson that sometimes it's cooler to just be honest about how you're feeling and actually let someone know you're hurt than attempt an elaborate stunt and end up with two very uncool broken arms.

People who block the baggage carousel at the airport

The airport is essentially made up of a collection of strangers who are either about to be trapped on, or have just escaped from, a long tube hurtling through the sky. If the tube were to crash, the results would be catastrophic. Thankfully, most of the time it doesn't. Still, no matter how seasoned a flyer you are, the possibility is always lurking in the back of your mind. So you end up with a bunch of people who don't even realise they are in a heightened emotional state, with somewhere pressing to be, sometimes with kids in tow, often sleep-deprived, having paid sixteen dollars for one of the worst sandwiches they've ever eaten in their entire life and spent several minutes trying to convince security that they're not carrying an explosive device, all forced together into a confined space. (And speaking of security, why do we have to take our jackets off when we walk through the X-ray? Can it not see through the jacket?)

This combination of people and behaviours can be enough to trigger 200 EPMs (eyerolls per minute). It's not uncommon to see people hurtling towards their departure gate with a McDonald's bag flapping in the breeze, having held up an entire plane full of people just because they couldn't resist the temptation of a Big Mac. Then you've got the middle-aged men wearing wraparound Oakley sunglasses who take nearly fifteen minutes to put their luggage in the overhead compartment because they're trying to not squash the twelve-pack of Krispy Kreme donuts they've bought, with no thought whatsoever to the line of people behind them trying to get to their seats. Sometimes you're seated next to an older gentleman who takes advantage of the fact that you are legally required to be strapped in and, for the next several hours, forces you to listen to his perspective on the world and all that's wrong with it – it's the hostage situation the airline industry refuses to talk about.

In my early twenties, I lived with a friend who was a stripper. She would come home exhausted, not just from dancing but also from what she described as the emotional labour of talking to the regulars who came to the club just looking for some company. She said a lot of the money she made was from simply widening her eyes as though she was listening and agreeing vehemently with whatever the man said. I personally have no idea what it's like to be an escort or a stripper, but I do feel like I've experienced a small part of their job when I too am being forced to smile, nod and remember when to blink my eyes as a man in the seat next to me drones on and on. I wait for the end of that plane trip the way a stripper waits for the last few chords of 'Sweet Cherry Pie' to ring out into the night. At least strippers, like my friend, get paid at the end of their interaction. My only payment is that, once I walk off the plane, I get to not smell halitosis.

There's the entitled businesswoman who makes you feel like a monster for sitting next to her in your assigned seat, the smug looks from the boomers in business class as you walk past them, and the long lines for the bathroom. There's also the constant fear of missing your flight and the at times unforgiving nature of the people whose job it is to help you navigate the entire process. Plus, there are kids everywhere who think they're cuter than they are, when in reality they've just reminded you that you've only got a couple more hours to take that morning-after pill.

Then once you've reached your destination there are the people who apparently want their bags more than everyone else, since they've decided to wait so close to the baggage carousel that no one else can reach or even see their bags coming around.

As easy as it is to get frustrated by people at the airport, it can be worth taking a moment to consider why they are there in the first place. Sometimes the reason you're at the airport is a good one, like a fabulous overseas holiday. But sometimes it's a bad one, like having to travel to a loved one's funeral. I realised that the only way to get through airports without losing my mind is to try to imagine the inner lives of the people who recline their seats during a one-hour flight, because you never know if they've been up all night with their sick mum and this flight was their only chance to get a quick nap in before returning to work or family life.

So thank you to the people who block the baggage carousel at the airport. In order to free myself from the frustration you cause me, I've worked harder to treat people with compassion, and to see them as complex individuals rather than how I used to see them: as self-centred, khaki short–wearing Krispy Kreme consumers, whose only mission in life was to annoy me, the main protagonist of the airport, Becky Lucas.

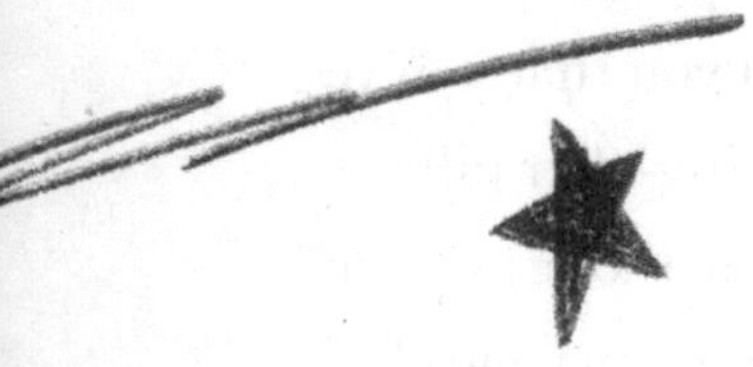

Isabella

When I first moved to Sydney in 2013, at age twenty-four, I lived in an apartment block high above a busy road in the inner-city suburb that everyone lives in when they first move to Sydney.

Newtown is a bustling place where everyone has a septum piercing and cool hair, thinks everything they're doing is terribly important, wears clothes that were obviously targeted to them on Instagram, and talks loudly and opinionatedly about things they don't actually know that much about.

'It's like they've never even heard of restorative justice,' a girl will say to her friend, having just learnt the term 'restorative justice'.

I loved living there. At the time, I fit right in. But now that I'm older, it's cringey to see the new generation of people you used to be like. They remind me of the dumb things I said at twenty-four, and who needs that?

I shared an apartment with my two friends Jaime and Simon, and my bedroom was on the side facing the busy street. The room also had a window shaped like a circle that was impossible to put a curtain over. My room, therefore, was impossibly bright and loud – two elements that I feel can really tip you into full-blown psychosis if endured for long enough.

What was good about Newtown, though, is that no matter how mental you appeared, there was always someone nearby to take the focus off you. Like the homeless man who wore steampunk goggles and would stand underneath my window, chanting about the dangers of gay people from 3 am to around 8 am. The worst thing about this was that his chants were quite catchy, and I'd regularly find myself in line for coffee in my very forward-thinking, progressive neighbourhood, singing his homophobic ear worms. Isn't it funny what sticks with you? I could still recite some of it now, but I can't remember a single conversation I ever had with my grandma.

I liked how I felt during those days of living there. I distinctly remember walking along the street with the sun on my face, feeling really happy for no apparent reason. I guess it was just because I was young and hopeful. I'm still hopeful now, but it's a different type of hope when you're older – you hope there's parking at your destination, you hope you don't randomly develop a gluten allergy. Life, once exciting and full of possibilities, becomes something you must navigate with as much ease as possible.

I walked a lot back then, mostly in the interest of finding money, which was needed to bridge the gap between the days when my Centrelink payment ran out and when the next payment went into my account. It sounds so pathetic, looking for money on the street, but I did quite often find some – at least fifty cents, which would be enough for a packet of ramen noodles. And if my roommates weren't home, I could nick one of their tins of tuna to have with it, and coast off that until dinner.

It was while I lived in this place that I saw my first dead body. It happened after I'd come ambling back into the apartment, having snuck into an afternoon movie session at the Dendy cinema, which was very easy to do back then. My roommate Simon pointed out an ambulance tent that had been set up in the alley beside our building. I popped my head out of the window and, sure enough, there was a big white tent with ambulance officers standing there, all looking in different directions. There was a body-sized lump on the road, covered with a sheet, and a shoe lying not far away from the lump, which I assumed belonged to the person who was lying underneath the sheet.

That shoe stood out to me, because the first thing I thought was 'I had that shoe' – it was one of those basic black ballet flats you might buy from Novo, Payless or, should you be so lucky, Wittner. For a couple years there, girls my age persisted with these horrific little flats, despite the fact that we were constantly slipping out of them and having to put Band-Aids over our blisters. I'm always so pleased to see the younger generation of girls are smart enough to have figured out they can just wear Converse sneakers or literally anything else.

We didn't know why there was a dead body on the ground outside our building but, I tell you what, there is nothing quite like it to lift you out of the malaise of being hungry and unemployed. At first, we thought it might have been a local who had overdosed, or a murder victim who had been unceremoniously dumped there.

Eventually, the sight of a white tent, a sheet-covered lump and a shoe got a bit dull, so we pulled our heads back in and turned on the television, taking turns to occasionally put our head out the window for a dead-body update. After several turns, I looked down to see, not a white tent, lump and shoe like I had so many times before, but the full confronting vision of the dead body of what looked like an older woman, though it was hard to know for sure. I guess bodies go flat when they fall from big heights. I had never thought about that before then.

Over the coming days, our intrigue turned to sadness and then back to curiosity. We wanted to find out more about her, but none of our neighbours had any information about what had happened or who she was.

As luck would have it, I bumped into the building's real estate agent in the lift, who told me the full story. He said that the woman's name was Isabella, and she had lived in the penthouse apartment with her husband, John, for twenty years. John had been an inventor who'd had some success in the 1980s with his designs, and so they were financially very comfortable. They were both seventy-nine years old and had no kids. They had been madly in love almost their entire lives and had barely spent a day apart, up until a few months ago when John had died. He had been working on a high-speed electric bike and, during a test drive, he lost control and rode the bike at full speed into a brick wall, suffering injuries that led to his death soon after.

In the following months, Isabella fell into a deep depression. Her community of friends did their best to take care of her, but they weren't up to the task – not just emotionally but also physically. With no kids to help her with the things John used to take care of, and Isabella talking constantly of wanting to kill herself, the real estate agent convinced her to move into a retirement home where she could meet other people her age and attempt to enjoy her remaining years. He explained to her that the price she could get for her apartment would ensure a very comfortable existence in a home (and a tidy little commission for him too, I imagine).

The real estate agent told me he had been helping Isabella find somewhere suitable. They'd visited a few nursing homes and she was starting to come around to the idea and was even feeling optimistic about it all.

The day of the move, he had been helping her to pack up her things into boxes. I've personally never been able to get a real estate agent to even return my calls, but maybe he was just one of the good ones.

He told me that, as they were pulling away in the car, she had turned to him and said in a panicked voice that she'd forgotten something upstairs, something personal John had given her. The real estate agent gave her the keys and said he'd wait downstairs in the car while she went up and did what she needed to do.

Isabella, I'm glad the first dead body I saw was yours, as you sounded really cool. And you may just have succeeded in making a real estate agent feel guilty, perhaps for the first time ever.

Emma

When I was sixteen, one of my best friends' mum got married to an Englishman. He was an acceptable-enough guy, but I never fully connected with him. It could have had something to do with the fact that he played the clarinet, an instrument so boring I believe the human brain is unable to think about it for more than three seconds before shutting down, or because of the way he pronounced the word 'yoghurt'. Either way, I remember feeling that the marriage could never be a long-term thing.

However, what did excite me was the prospect of an impending visit from his English daughter, who my best friend Amrita and I decided was going to be our new best friend. Her name was Emma and she was about two years older than us, which obviously meant she was pure perfection. We became obsessed with knowing everything about her even before we'd laid eyes on her.

The day she landed in Australia, I arrived breathless from my bike ride, clearly far too eager. As soon as I was introduced to her, I sensed her immediately recoil from me and that pretty much set the tone for the rest of her visit.

This girl, who we'd had such high hopes for, couldn't have been less interested in us. She would wake up in the morning and fix herself a cup of tea and toast, then retire to her room where she would spend hours on the phone talking loudly with her friends back home. We'd listen by her door as she'd say, 'Oh yeah … Yeah … Yeah, of course, absolutely! Oh my god, I know. I mean, I'm sorry if this sounds bad, but there's a reason Australia is separated from the rest of the world.' And then she'd laugh in this way that suggested she wasn't actually sorry if she sounded bad.

Emma was the first person who I'd ever heard use the expression 'Murphy's Law'. She was always saying it. Someone would stub their toe on the bitumen and she'd lazily declare in her raspy British voice, 'Well, it's Murphy's Law, isn't it?' I'd agree, even though I couldn't figure out what it meant based on the way she was using the expression.

There is something hilarious about people using their native language incorrectly, especially British people, who went around the world insisting that everyone speak English. In 2013, my friend Anna, who was stoned at the time, confessed that she wasn't quite sure that she knew what the word 'sarcasm' meant. I explained it as best I could and watched her face as it dawned on her that she may have been using the word incorrectly. She admitted to me that she had thought it meant saying mean things that are true but pretending you're joking. I began mentally flicking back through all her 'sarcastic comments' and wanting to curl up into a ball and die.

Most of the time, Emma didn't want anything to do with Amrita and me, but, occasionally, when the time difference meant her friends back home had gone to sleep, she'd get bored and give us a puff on her cigarette and show us messages that boys back in England had sent her.

Emma's disdain for us was nothing personal; she mostly just had it in for Australia. Amrita and her mum and now stepdad lived up in the hinterland in an eco-house, which was designed in such a way that even though you were inside, you felt as though you were outside. Their house was full of bugs, geckos and other sorts of wildlife, and there was really nothing you could do to avoid it. It had a drop toilet, which meant that every week her mum would have to empty out a large bucket filled with urine and faeces that didn't come from her. I was never fully comfortable with the idea of this, and I used to wonder whether the fact that she had to face the excrement of every person who crossed the threshold of her home meant she was choosier with her friends. If this made me feel squeamish, I could only imagine how Emma the English Rose felt about it all.

It all reached a climax one day. We were sitting around in the lounge room, discussing what to do that day, and Emma started complaining for the hundredth time about Australia and why it was so bad. She tearfully told us she didn't want to go on a bushwalk; she didn't want to go to the beach; and she was sick of the spiders, the midges and the geckos.

She asked her dad if she could go back to England earlier than they'd arranged.

He said no.

She started yelling at him about the unfair living conditions she was putting up with, about how they lived 'like animals'. Back home, she said, she had her sheets cleaned almost daily! Ironed as well!

She said that she couldn't help but think about the snakes. She was terrified, and how could her dad be okay with his daughter being scared every day of her life?

Her dad tried to calm her down, telling her that there were no snakes, which only set her off even more.

'There are snakes! There are!' she screamed. 'How dare you tell me there aren't snakes! We're living in the fucking outback!'

It was absolutely not the outback, but I wasn't about to pipe up.

The hysterics continued while we all watched on. I probably should have left, really. After a few moments, we noticed a fine dust starting to sprinkle down on her, lightly at first. Then, before we had time to process what was happening, there was a loud crack. We all looked up to see the ceiling above us starting to cave in and, from the exposed gap, a huge three-metre carpet snake fell and landed on Emma's neck, then her lap, and eventually the floor, where it coiled up, no doubt pretty startled by what had just happened.

I don't really remember what happened after that. I do recall there being a lot of screaming and crying on Emma's part, and I think someone did say 'Blimey' at one point.

But at least Emma finally learnt what the expression 'Murphy's Law' meant.

So thank you to Emma for showing me what Murphy's Law meant in such an entertaining way. I'll never forget it.

Heather's dad

I don't remember what my friend Heather's dad did for a living, but if I were to say he was a door-to-door salesman, then I think that would get my point across. He constantly wore the expression of a man who was regularly told 'no'.

Heather's mum wanted to leave Heather's dad, but could never fully commit to it. She'd leave on the weekend and then return on Tuesday to drink white wine on the couch. I once walked into their bedroom and saw him on his knees, giving his wife a Brazilian wax. Even at age fourteen, I knew that you would never ask a man you were truly in love with to do that.

Heather was incredible at making girls at school cry. She had this sneer that could have anyone in a heap from existential angst, questioning why they'd ever tried anything in their entire life when they were such a worthless worm.

I still think about her sneer and whether she's currently putting it to good use.

They were a funny lot, this family. There were four kids: Heather, Sacha, Michael and Stan. They all seemed like lab experiments gone wrong, with very thin translucent skin and weak chins. Children already have an incredible ability to sniff out someone's insecurity, and these siblings were better than most. And the person they loved to torment the most was their dad. He just couldn't get his kids to respect him. It was so bad that whoever was over at their house that day would often partake in the mockery as well. I didn't want to gang up on Heather's dad, but if everyone else was doing it, it was just easier to join in.

On Friday afternoons, there was a Samoan man who would sell fireworks to kids at the back of the school oval. Michael and Stan would buy some, head home and then tape their dad's belongings to individual rockets and set them off. He'd come home, already defeated from work, to see one of his shoes sailing through the afternoon sky.

'Come on, kids,' he'd wearily mutter.

It got to be so much that Heather's dad enlisted the help of a therapist, which was strange. No one had a therapist where I grew up. If you were upset, you either drank, silently fished off the jetty or developed stomach cancer over forty years of holding it all in (or all three). But off he went, every week, to see this therapist woman who I doubt could ever truly understand what these kids were capable of.

On a day when we were supposed to be at school but instead had chosen to lie on mattresses on the floor watching TV, Michael came into the lounge room, smiling and holding a notebook. It was a diary that was being kept by their dad, obviously as an exercise prescribed to him by his therapist.

A huge mistake.

We flicked through the pages like frenzied animals.

Tuesday 15th of April
4.30 pm: Asked Heather nicely if she would feed the cat while I was out, her response was 'get fucked'.
10.40 pm: Sacha told me the dishes would be done before she went to bed. Guess who ended up doing them?

Wednesday 16th of April
3.40 pm: Asked Michael how school was and he farted at me.

Thursday 17th April
7.30 am: Dan popped a party popper in my face. Didn't seem concerned for my safety in the slightest.

We gathered around the notebook like it was some kind of sacrosanct artefact that had been given to us by the gods of comedy. Then we realised what we had to do. We started making fake entries in the back half of the diary for him to eventually find. Things like:

> *4th of June*
> 3.50 pm: Did a big poopy shit in my underpants. God it's everywhere. Running down my leg oh no.
>
> *13th of July*
> 7.30 pm: Not again! What is wrong with my bum? So much poo. Dear god. My ass.
>
> *4th of August*
> 8 am: I'm a dumb cunt.

The next couple of weeks nearly killed us as we watched him surreptitiously write his diary entries, not realising we were all breathlessly waiting for him to find ours.

A few weeks later, Heather came to school and told us her dad finally came across the diary entries we'd written. She said he'd come into the lounge room and asked them when they'd found the diary. When they told him, he stood up and wordlessly left the house. That had been a few days ago, and Heather's dad still hadn't come back.

Heather didn't seem that concerned. She said he was probably staying at his mum's place.

Then, that Friday afternoon, he'd apparently walked through the door with a bit more colour in his face and a spring in his step, ready to accept a few apologies from the kids.

Michael briefly looked up from his Game Boy and said, 'Gay shirt,' which, according to Heather, caused her mum to spit out her wine from laughter.

Thank you to Heather's dad for the reminder that you should never write anything down that you don't want to be read. It's not worth it.

Ros

Stand-up comedy can be terrifying. When I'm nervous or scared, I don't really like to talk to people I don't know before a show, yet that's exclusively what happens. It's bizarre – you're about to do this thing that for most people would be their worst nightmare, but you're also expected to have light playful banter with whomever is around, lest you be labelled rude by a venue manager in regional Queensland.

When you are doing shows away from home, there's usually someone who comes and picks you up from your hotel or wherever you're staying to take you to the venue, which is very nice of the organisers and all, but the last thing you feel like doing before performing onstage is making polite chitchat with some driver you'll never see again. I'm sure they don't want to talk to me either. Most of the time I feel like we're both just sitting there, wearily passing the conversational baton back and forth, secretly yearning for silence.

In Perth, I got chatting to this driver who was a gruff old man, and I liked him immediately. I've always liked men who aren't concerned with how they come across to others, because it feels like they're not trying to hide anything. Whenever there's a documentary about a serial killer, there's usually a scene with their mum, sitting in a faded floral lounge chair, tearfully explaining that she doesn't know how any of this happened, that her son wouldn't even hurt a fly, and I've always thought, *Well, maybe that's because he was exhausted from murdering women.* That's why nothing makes me feel safer than a guy who, when faced with a crackling brown cockroach, proceeds to squash it dead with his shoe.

In my industry, I constantly see the nice guy who shares all the right articles and parrots the safe popular opinion come undone every time, because of course they do. Let's not forget that one of the nicest, cleanest comedians was Bill Cosby. When someone is so obsessed with seeming like a good person who never puts a foot wrong, I can't help but wonder why. To me, a person who seems so intent on seeming nice all of the time is obviously insecure in their goodness and perhaps, deep down, even a bit scared of their own thoughts. A little insider tip: a lot of the people you see in the public eye who consistently say the right things are actually the ones to look out for.

As I was sitting there enjoying this curmudgeonly man's

conversation, I happened to glance down and see that he had a Southern Cross tattoo on his leg. *Goddamit*, I thought.

Then I saw he was watching me look at his leg. He paused for a moment, then said, 'It's not like that, like, what you're … thinking it is.'

I asked him what he meant.

He explained that when he was younger, the Southern Cross tattoo wasn't a symbol of nationalism, nor had it had any racist connotations. He told me he got it when he was travelling overseas with a group of hippies, to whom the tattoo was merely a representation of the collection of stars found in the Southern Hemisphere sky, which reminded them of home when they were so far away. He told me that back when he was young, if you had one of these tattoos, it was actually a sign that you were progressive, that you saw all of humanity as one living under the same stars. To be honest, it sounded pretty lame to me, though I was pleased I hadn't wasted good conversation on an old racist.

I thought how much it must have sucked for him to be sitting there with a Southern Cross tattoo, watching the Cronulla riots and sensing what his tattoo would come to represent. Who knows what we're all sporting these days that might get co-opted by a racist movement. It could be anything, really – maybe my grandkid will be thumbing through a photo album and shriek at the sight of me and my friends wearing Kathmandu jackets. 'You don't understand, we all had one, it was colder then,' I'll protest through my (fingers crossed) drug haze.

It did make me feel better about having not once being trendy or ahead of my time; as I've mentioned somewhere in this book, it's always taken me longer than most to get with the program. I mean, I am only now just considering a bucket hat.

Being ahead of your time seems hard. Sylvia Plath was, and she ended up sticking her head in an oven. I have a friend whose dad started an online environmental store in 1997, which flopped. He went on to own a business that made customised jigsaw puzzles based on photographs that you could order as gifts for friends and family. Neither of these businesses took off, because the public simply wasn't ready for them at the time. What's worse, you don't get credit for having done it first – only if you make it work. Had he started these businesses ten or twenty years later, he'd probably be a multi-millionaire by now.

I often think about Galileo and his discovery that the Earth revolves around the Sun rather than the other way around, which resulted in the church accusing him of heresy and jailing him for a large portion of his adult life. It must be quite lonely to be ahead of the curve; it's like loving an obscure TV show that no one else has heard of and with whom there's no one to talk to about it. Poor Galileo would have attended dinner parties with people who still happily believed the Sun revolved around the Earth and he would have spent hours chewing their ear off, trying to get them to listen to him, ignoring the pointed glances they were giving to their friend nearby in a plea to save them. It's not fun to be the person who knows more than everyone else, yet there is pressure to be original and to stand out and to be the first. So where does that leave us? With a bunch of people who all sort of know the same thing, but a few of them are wearing cool hats.

I worked at a law firm when I was eighteen or maybe nineteen – what's the difference, anything before twenty-five doesn't matter. Besides comedy, every other job I've had I've either been fired from or just found myself being slowly phased out by management. I'm quite bad at understanding how things work; I really do believe I'm missing some of the basic skills in life, but what those skills are exactly, I'm not sure.

Every task they gave me at the law firm I was unable to understand or complete satisfactorily, to a degree where I shocked even myself. I was known for doing photocopies the wrong way around before crucial court appearances, filing things away so they were unable to be found later, leaking personal information to clients over the phone, and I believe at one point I implied one of the partners looked a lot older than her age.

My saving grace was Ros the legal secretary, who was this small older lady that wore the most darling outfits. She had big, beautiful, sad eyes, but if you didn't know her son had died, you wouldn't call them sad, just beautiful. I was supposed to be helping her, but she figured out pretty early on that I wasn't really up to the task. She liked me nonetheless. She would tell me things about her life in a very composed way and, mid-story, gently point out something I'd bungled without making me feel bad about it.

One afternoon, as I was counting down the minutes until I could leave, there was a knock on the office door. Ros went to answer it, something that I now realise probably fell more into my job description. In came one of the local homeless men, Paul, who would sell pencils and little butterfly clips he made himself to nearby businesses, and who one summer gave me a fantastic tip about drinking celery juice to keep cool.

Paul bustled in past Ros, opened his suitcase where he kept his wares and ran through his usual spiel, outlining the cost of each pencil and what packages would be the best value. Paul always had a healthy amount of saliva on his face, so while he delivered this quite wet sales pitch, we both stood politely out of spray's reach until he ran out of steam.

Ros then declared enthusiastically that she'd like two boxes of pencils, handed him a twenty-dollar note and he at once began busying himself with his latest purchase order. Once the transaction was complete, Ros walked him back to the front door, as she would any client or visitor, and thanked him for the lovely pencils. In that moment, it all just got too much for him and he burst into a huge smile and gave her a big sloppy kiss on the cheek.

I had stayed back in the reception, hidden behind the door frame so she didn't know I could see them. I watched as she stood there with saliva all over her dainty little cheek and wished him a nice day. Once he'd left, she closed the door with a smile, reached into her pocket, took out her handkerchief and wiped Paul's spit off her face.

I know what she did shouldn't be that groundbreaking, but it was to me. I knew if he had kissed me like that, I would have instinctively wiped my face immediately, and there would have been a part of me that thought that was okay because he was homeless and probably wouldn't notice, and even if he did, who really cared.

I told my dad about Ros and what I'd seen her do.

'You know,' he said, 'it's okay to take the bits from people that you like and incorporate them into your own personality. Nobody's original, it's all been done before, so you might as well give up trying to be unique and instead just learn from others and take on the behaviours that seem like they're working.' He shrugged, seemingly completely unaware how radical this advice was.

This went against everything Western culture seems to tell us about individuality. Every advertisement for clothing or makeup is about 'finding the real you', reinvention, showing others you aren't afraid to stand out or go against the grain. But, really, there is so much beauty and knowledge to be gleaned from the people and ideas that already populate our communities.

For me, one of the hardest pills I have had to swallow is that every cliché or truism I had rejected when I was younger as being reductive or obvious or 'not original' has more or less ended up being the perfect way to encapsulate nearly every experience I've ever had.

When you're younger, you can't believe a simple expression like 'Be careful what you wish for' could ever hold within its words the life lessons you are on a quest for. But these little sayings do – that's why they are still around thousands of years later.

I suppose these sayings came about because people got sick of having to tell an entire story every time they wanted to pass on a life lesson, so they summed up the lesson into a simple cliché that could be passed down to people in a matter of seconds, in an attempt to help others not make the same mistakes they did. But personally, I have continued to ignore the lessons told to me in clichés, until I have bitterly experienced for myself why that cliché is actually true. (Ironically, this is summed up in another cliché: I had to 'learn the hard way'.)

The idea that all the wisdom I eventually amassed after years of agony can be summed up in phrases people get tattooed on their bodies after drinking six cans of rum and Coke has the effect of making me feel small and insignificant. But lately I've started to realise that it shouldn't make me feel that way. If anything, I should see these little wisdom gems as incredible examples of how human beings want to share the ways they've learnt how to minimise human suffering.

When you think about it, clichés are actually the vocalisations of a shared collective consciousness.

Actually, I think that sentence would make a pretty cool tattoo.

So thank you to Ros for a small lesson in what it means to really treat someone with dignity and compassion. I took that part of you and tried my best to make it mine.

Nick Wiley

The first time I was properly broken up with was at age seventeen by a boy named Nick Wiley. Even before he dumped me, I had sensed he didn't want to be with me anymore, so I'd been dodging his calls for days. I figured that he couldn't break up with me if he never got the chance to talk to me! So when he finally got through to me and asked if I would come over, I knew deep down what was about to happen. Still, there was a large part of me that was in denial, so I did my hair and makeup anyway and tried to pretend that maybe he did just want to hang out. With hope in my heart, I walked to his house.

I had been in love with Nick since I was five years old and, after a lifetime of pining over him, I was never completely comfortable in his presence. He was the son of one of my mum's musician friends, two years older than me, and I only ever got to see him once or twice a year when our parents would get together. By the time I was a teenager, I was constantly in a state of either 'about to see Nick' or 'having just seen Nick'. Every free moment was spent thinking about him, to the point that most of the things I did and learnt were in part motivated by wanting him to find out what I'd done or learnt. It's embarrassing how many hobbies I've taken up simply on the off-chance a boy I like might see me doing it well and love me for it. The most cringeworthy example being the year I took up and was, like, into fire-twirling.

When I was younger, the crush I had on Nick was more innocent. I used to get nervous around him, but when I wasn't in his presence I forgot to think about him. It was when I was thirteen and he kissed me in a dark room that started everything – for me, that is. I can say with complete confidence that he wouldn't have thought about that kiss again for the rest of his life.

For the next couple of years, I spent a lot of my time lying in the sun with my head resting on my forearms, staring into the grass and imagining what it would be like to be with Nick. We'd have imaginary conversations where I would dazzle him with my intelligence and wit, because in these scenarios it was always me doing the talking, which goes to show how much being in love with someone is really mostly about you rather than them.

I had never felt these feelings of obsession about someone who I was actually around every now and then. Every time I'd see him, I couldn't wait to get home to my bed so I could remember everything he'd said and every interaction we'd had. I'd replay them in my head over and over again, until my brain did that thing it does where the memory alters itself ever so slightly (yes, now that I think about it, his hand *did* brush up against mine on purpose). Content with my delusion, I'd fall asleep.

My main reason for wanting a phone at age fourteen was so I could text him, but my mum was against me having one, so I had to get creative. I ended up concocting an elaborate scenario where I genuinely locked myself out of the house for hours on end and made it seem like it was my mum's fault for not being able to communicate the location of the spare key.

'It's just a safety issue – anything could have happened to me locked out of the house for so long,' I explained to her, my powers of manipulation already fairly strong by that age. 'Things like this could be avoided if you let me have a phone.'

Once I got the phone, I feverishly sent Nick a very relaxed message on MSN Messenger, letting him know I had a phone now and that he should 'shoot me his number' – just one of those casual expressions we use to disguise psychotic behaviour. Like the time an ex-boyfriend waited until my roommates had left, broke into my house and trapped me in the bathroom threatening to kill me, before my mum thankfully pulled up to the house in her little Holden Barina to take me to lunch. The ex-boyfriend then sent me a message days later, apologising for 'rocking up unannounced'. In general, I think the expression 'rocking up unannounced' should be reserved for when a man turns up to a party uninvited with a carton of beer on his shoulder, not a break-and-enter.

Once I had my phone and access to Nick, I found myself in text exchanges with him that lasted days. I'd agonise over my replies and read way too much into the things he said – though, to be fair, his messages often did verge on flirtatious. I've heard so many people say that women shouldn't waste time on men who clearly aren't into us, but, honestly, what a treat to be seventeen, on the precipice of euphoric love, and completely vulnerable. One day I'll be seventy-eight and wishing that I could muster up the energy to message a boy for hours.

I generally agree with the sentiment that life is short and you shouldn't stress out about someone who probably won't matter to you in the future. But I also believe that a huge part of love and dating is the wasted time. The stress of composing a text and waiting for a reply, the giddiness of receiving one back, the not-knowing where it's all going to go – none of it feels like a waste to me. Eventually you will settle down or you won't, and that's cool either way, but regardless, the passion and neurosis and gut-wrenching feeling of texting with someone you're obsessed with is part of the fun. Often, being with them in real life is a complete let-down. So I say enjoy the texting, and know that even if you do end up wasting your time, you still got to experience the best part of love: the anticipation.

One Friday night, during a particularly frenzied text session, Nick told me he was going to be busking in the Valley

Mall on Saturday morning and I should 'come hang'. I began planning my outfit in my head as I messaged him saying that I'd do my best.

I spent that whole Saturday wandering the city alone from 9 am to 4 pm keeping a lookout for him, while also trying to seem like I had things to do in the city in case he saw me from afar.

I waited in line for a Krispy Kreme donut, which was something people did a lot in Brisbane. For a while there, you couldn't get Krispy Kreme donuts unless a visiting relative brought them for you from Sydney or Melbourne. Thanks to this novelty, the first Krispy Kreme store in Brisbane constantly had a line and that made them seem so … exclusive. This may be another false memory, but I'm seventy per cent sure that at one point there was even a red velvet rope at the entrance of the store.

After I'd done that, I really didn't have a lot more to do, and my vagina was starting to chafe. I'd made a strange last-minute decision to shave it for the first time in my life and I didn't know exactly what I was doing. I think I missed a few sections of hair, which created a rough, abrasive situation that made it difficult for me to walk.

Eventually I had to give up. I was already running late and would be in trouble if I didn't check in with Mum soon, so I got on the bus home.

As we were pulling away from the stop, I received a message from Nick that read, 'Hey! How was your day? Ended up not busking … couldn't be fucked haha.'

And I sat there smiling so hard my face hurt. The fact that he'd thought to message me meant that the whole day had been worth it.

There was eventually a second hookup that happened on one of our parents' camping trips, just a couple of months before he was due to graduate from high school. I spent a few more months living off that memory, but I was starting to wonder whether I'd ever see him again. He had graduated, after all, and was now living in the real world, no longer obligated to attend family parties or holidays, which were just about the only times I ever saw him. Our text messages had become few and far between and he was constantly about to move to Melbourne or even overseas with his friends.

The only pieces of information I could gather were from Nick's vague Myspace updates or from overheard conversations between my mum and her friends. This was always a dangerous game as they had no idea how much I loved him, so I was privy to information that hadn't been run through a filter aimed at protecting my feelings. I'd be sitting at the kitchen table and one of my mum's friends would casually mention that Nick had a new girlfriend. Then six months later, I'd find myself sitting at the same table eating a cream finger bun and hear that they'd broken up, at which an evil smile would dance across my sugar-frosted lips.

Then something truly miraculous happened. My mum ran into Nick busking outside of the shops near where I lived.

He told her he was broke and that the move to Melbourne hadn't been as smooth as he would have liked, which was why he had come back to Brisbane. There must be a surplus of optimism in the brains of musicians who move to big cities to pursue their art. There's typically only a short amount of time between the moment you get off at Central Station, guitar case in hand, spinning around in wonderment at the Big Smoke, and the moment you realise you have no more money in your bank account and that, actually, Ben Harper covers probably aren't going to cut the mustard.

Upon hearing Nick's plight, my mum told him he was welcome to come and live with us rent free until he got back on his feet.

Even though I felt bad that Nick was having trouble financially, I couldn't deny that this was really quite an unbelievable turn of events for me. My forever crush was moving into my actual house where I could get to him whenever I pleased, and I thought that was just great.

Within a couple of weeks of living together and forcing occasional hookups, I wore him down into officially becoming my boyfriend. I suppose he felt bad for living rent free in our home and not making an honest woman out of me. So he begrudgingly let me call him my boyfriend and did the bare minimum that a boyfriend would do, and that was, as they say, good enough for me.

After a couple of months of living with us, he moved into a

share house not too far from us, just up the street, left for five blocks and right up the hill.

The day he broke up with me, I stood outside his house, already nervous about seeing his twenty-something-year-old roommates. They were these two gorgeous Brazilian girls with bouncy hair, perfect skin and womanly bodies, who had both treated me with pity the last couple of times I had come over.

Through the window, I could see Nick sitting at his kitchen table. He clocked me standing outside, poised to walk up the stairs into the house, and jumped up out of his chair and walked down to meet me, presumably to try to intercept me and prevent me from coming inside and making a scene in front of his friends.

The flat he lived in had a communal area underneath where there were some old couches and candles and other bohemian party artefacts. I wasn't surprised when he asked me to go downstairs with him; it was a great place to break up with someone. And he was definitely breaking up with me, because he'd never been so attentive and present before.

The most painful thing for me in that moment was watching the person I loved breathe a sigh of relief that they finally did not have to spend time with me anymore. I resented being the subject of what no doubt would have been a household discussion about what he was about to do and how he was going to do it. He held my hand as he delivered a spiel about not being in the right place for a relationship. My lip started trembling the way they do in cartoons. I couldn't control it no matter how hard I tried, and it became my main focus, instead of listening to Nick dance around the reasons he didn't like me, which I already knew. I instead just kept trying to not let my lip tremble.

At the end of it, he asked me if I had any questions.

I said, 'No, all good, that's fine,' and continued tensing my lip hard against my teeth.

Afterwards, he gave me one of those big disgusting hippy hugs where they push their heart against yours, absolving himself of his guilt, and then walked me back up to the top of the street. I waved goodbye, then sobbed my heart out for the entire way home, my bottom lip now completely out of control.

I was so sad that it felt otherworldly, but there was also an underlying sense of relief. It's tiring knowing someone doesn't love you back and there's only so long you can do it to yourself. It wasn't long, though, before the clarity of that revelation subsided and was replaced by a hard move into denial, where I began to convince myself that he'd eventually want me back.

I gave him many opportunities to figure this out and threw myself in front of him as often as I could. In the last few months of high school, I found myself walking down his street on my way home from school ever so slowly, hoping to run into him. I must have made my mum detour past his place thousands of times, so I could try to get a peek inside his house and see who he was kissing nowadays. I stood at the back of concert halls and gigs I knew he was performing at and hung around afterwards, knowing that basic manners would force him to come over and say hello. I didn't care that he wasn't talking to me by choice. I was addicted to trying to make him love me.

My younger sister Hannah called me the other day and asked my advice on how to play it cool in front of a boy who had rejected her. Before I could stop myself, I let out a laugh, which I immediately felt bad about – just because I'm old and emotionally calloused, doesn't mean she is yet. I realised that for her and other young people, there is this idea that there is a solution to all of life's problems out there and they just have to find it. My sister has been able to order Ubers since she was fifteen; she can look up the answer to almost anything on the internet; and if there's something more complex she doesn't know or fully understand, she can watch YouTube videos that will feed her opinions she can use as her own.

I didn't want to have to be the one to tell her that there is not and has never been a way to successfully play it cool around a guy you care about. You could not look at them all night and it would still seem glaringly obvious that you have feelings for them. The only time you will ever actually appear cool and aloof towards them is when you truly don't care about them anymore, and then you don't even get to enjoy it.

And that's what happened to me. You don't get a letter or a notification telling you that you're over someone. Sometimes you think you are and you'll try to test yourself by looking at their social media profile or putting yourself in their presence again, which is when you'll realise, no, those feelings are still there. But when they're *actually* gone, you don't even realise because you've forgotten to even think about it. After years of suffering and indignity, all of a sudden, it's over.

I realised it was over about eighteen months after we'd broken up. I was going to get something to eat with my mum and there he was, busking on the corner of two main streets, and I felt nothing. If anything, I was a little grossed out by his outfit, which was a loose hemp caftan paired with pants made from paisley patchwork. We didn't cross the road to talk to him and instead kept walking on our side of the street to our destination.

Okay, perhaps I wasn't *completely* unmoved by the sight of him. It's similar to when I see a Krispy Kreme donut with a 'Quick sale' sticker on it, haphazardly displayed on the counter of a 7-Eleven. I know Krispy Kreme donuts have lost their cultural currency, but I can still remember what it felt like to really want them.

There's a deep feeling of melancholy when you realise you aren't in love with someone anymore. While it's a relief to not be held prisoner by the idea of them, there is a sense of, *Okay, well, what now? What do I think about when the bus is late, or when I can't fall asleep?* There's also the fear that perhaps they're the last person you'll ever have strong feelings for, and maybe you'll never feel anything as intense again for the rest of your life.

By the time Mum and I were walking back to the car, Nick had just finished, and was putting cords and cables into little sections of his guitar case. Mum asked if he'd like a lift home and, looking pretty tired, he happily accepted her offer.

As we were nearing his house, I began tensing up, realising that, to his knowledge, Mum had never been to his place. Nick had no idea about the daily drive-bys I insisted Mum do right after the breakup. I knew it would look suspicious if she knew where he lived and, just because I was over him, that didn't mean I wanted him to know I'd driven down that road more times than I could count (or that I'd pissed on his car twice).

I couldn't explain any of this to my mum without Nick hearing me, so I tried my hardest to telepathically shoot her an urgent message. Maybe we were just in tune that day or perhaps my mum has had years of experience herself at trying to play it cool in front of guys. Whatever it was, I'll be forever grateful to her for finding his eyes in the rearview mirror and feigning confusion.

'Sorry, where is it? You'll have to direct me.'

Thank you to Nick for breaking up with me. I am open-minded, but there's just no way I could have married a busker.

Hens' parties

I've always hated the idea of hens' parties. I think it's their garish aesthetic – even when it's done ironically, it still makes me feel uneasy. Or maybe it's the idea that this is supposed to be the one 'final hurrah' for the bride-to-be, the 'last time' they'll do shots before vomiting into a bucket by 9 pm.

But the thing is, it's not really a final hurrah like it used to be, when women were sold off along with a cow and a good set of riding boots. Nowadays, even when you're married, you're still allowed out of the house for a night out (if you're lucky!). So, really, it just ends up being this fake celebration that you feel like you have to have fun at.

I don't like my fun being prescribed to me either. The idea that there is a time and place where we are all expected to get blind drunk and play games makes me immediately anxious.

The whole lead-up to it feels so unnatural – and it doesn't help that you're usually required to deposit large sums of money into some girl's bank account two weeks prior to the event. The girl organising the whole thing is always some girl you barely know, a wishy-washy work friend called Samantha who ends up planning four activities in one night, while you know you're going to be exhausted by the end of the first activity. For some reason, we all have to drink cocktails, even if that's not what you feel like, because 'They're fun!' So after a night of drinking five litres of sugar syrup blended up into a fruit purée while teetering around on high heels, you end up with a pounding headache and feeling acidic.

There also doesn't seem to be much point to the whole exercise. Traditionally, the idea of the hens' party was so women could share information on how to have a good marriage, and trade sex tips to keep their husbands happy. But since most hens aren't getting married until they're in their thirties these days, most of the attendees are either in admittedly shit marriages, still single or already divorced.

It also feels like a fake performative way of getting back at the boys for their raucous bucks' party, by insisting that we're having just as much horny and hedonistic fun with a male stripper. But, to me, it's not quite the same thing. The female body is just so beautiful that a girl writhing around in a G-string is objectively sexy for everyone, whereas when you see a man doing the same thing in a G-string, it makes you worry for him and his priorities.

And in my experience, concern does not usually facilitate the feeling of horniness. If a man I didn't know were to turn up and make me immediately horny, it wouldn't be from showing me his abs – my sexuality is more complicated than that. He would need to do something like help me download a TV show I can't find on any of the streaming services, or listen to a long and complicated story I'm telling and confirm that yes, I'm right, that person *is* an idiot.

However, just because I don't particularly like the idea of hens' parties, doesn't mean I haven't ever had a good time at one. There was one hens' party I went to years ago where, at one point in the night, I and four other girls had congregated at one area of the bar for a debrief. I've always wanted to be someone who can live in the moment, but unfortunately I fall into the category of 'person who needs to discuss and dissect everything going on around me as it happens'. During this crucial meeting of the minds, we were spotted by an older man who looked like he'd have a few travel tips if anyone were going to Thailand.

Now, I'm not usually the girl to point out a creep at the bar; in fact, I've always felt a bit left out whenever my friends complain that they've noticed a creep giving them the eye, because most of the time he hasn't given me any attention whatsoever. Sometimes I've felt so excluded that I've even contemplated flirting with him simply so I can join in on admonishing him along with everyone else.

For once though, it seemed like the creep was looking at *all* of us, which was really something! We felt his eyes on us as we continued to talk and managed to ignore him for about fifteen minutes until, mid-way through my sentence, I felt a tap on the shoulder. The creep had approached the group holding a tray of tequila shots he'd bought for us all.

None of us felt like a tequila shot, nor did we want to accept a drink from a man who might think we owed him five minutes of conversation in return. Plus he gave us the feeling that if we took the shots, we'd eventually find ourselves stepping forward as a group, pointing at him and tearfully clutching each other while saying in unison, 'Yes, your Honour, that's him. That's the man.'

We shooed him away as compassionately as possible, claiming we didn't like tequila. 'But thank you anyway, sir,' we said with the residual guilt that comes from saying no to a man who is offering you something.

He took the shots and walked back to his seat where he sat down and proceeded to do the five tequila shots all by himself. I remember thinking that this was much better entertainment than any male stripper could ever provide. A lonesome man at the bar downing nearly a quarter of a bottle of tequila to save face? Well … that was something that could make me horny.

Thank you to hens' parties for roping me into having 'fun' and providing me with a quintessential female experience I may not get to encounter if left to my own devices.

Stevie Nicks

In 2018, I saw Stevie Nicks in concert when she was touring Australia. I found myself captivated by the stories she would tell before she began singing. I loved listening to her acid-warped voice warbling on about her former flames, industry jealousies and drug-induced mental breakdowns. These stories made the following lyrics so much more revealing and intimate.

It was especially helpful for me, because she was doing a lot of stuff from her new album, which I hadn't listened to yet, and it usually takes me a few listens of any song to figure out if I like it or not. But with these little anecdotal introductions, I could focus less on whether I found the tune catchy and more on what the song was actually about. It's great fun as an audience member to hear a song sung by the person who actually wrote the lyrics, and to feel like you're being let in on a part of their life that meant so much to them that they were compelled to immortalise it in music.

I do wonder, though, whether it's as fun for the people who are being written about. Artists can't exist in a vacuum; their craft is dependent on the world around them. If you happen to cross paths with an artist who turns your interaction into art, it must feel infuriating to see entire audiences accept the artist's version of events – not even consciously but merely through the enraptured enjoyment of their art. It's the equivalent of someone you've had a falling out with, who also happens to possess the gift of persuasive storytelling, getting to the party first and explaining what happened between you two before you've arrived.

If somebody writes a song about you, there's no right of reply – and even if you do get the chance to explain yourself, what medium could ever trump a song? Let's say you did an interview on one of the world's most popular talk shows. It still wouldn't infiltrate people's minds the way a catchy song can. No couple will ever play your interview at their wedding or lip sync to it at karaoke while high on MDMA.

Now I think about it, it's possible I'm jealous that songwriters get to do a little preamble before their song. As a comedian, you can't really do the same thing with a joke. A joke typically has to be written to get the point across in the least amount of words possible, without losing so much context that it flops and, worse, people think you're a terrible person. It's incredible how important context is in making people feel comfortable with what you're saying.

There's a comedian I know who has an incredible capacity for understanding human nature and a genuine empathy that you don't see much of in my industry – both results of losing his parents at a young age and a lifetime spent working as a labourer to support his wife and kids. He is a man who does the right thing all the time and not just when he's being watched. Yet sometimes when he's onstage telling a joke that comes across as the musings of a typical sexist male comedian, I can see people in the crowd pulling away, not understanding that his gruffness is an act or that his jokes are dripping in irony. If they were able to hear his backstory or gain more insight into the way he writes, I believe he'd be considered one of the greatest comedians in the country. But then it wouldn't be a comedy show, it would be a storytelling night, and those are two very different things.

A friend of mine once brought a first date along to one of my shows where I told a joke I'd written years ago about orgasm inequality. After seeing the show, she told my friend that she thought I was sexist. I had written the joke after an extended period of what I felt was an unfair orgasm ratio between me and the men I was sleeping with. I went on to explain that I felt a sense of injustice at the fact that, as a woman, I not only seemed to be orgasming less than my male counterparts, but I was also the only one in our pairing who ran the risk of getting pregnant. I suggested that we develop some sort of technology that gave men the capacity to fall pregnant, so the risk of pregnancy was one that would be shared by both sexes. I then posed the idea that whoever orgasms first would then be the one who took on the risk. This, I reasoned, would incentivise men to make sure they weren't always the first to orgasm, because then they'd be the ones having to nip up to the pharmacist to get the morning-after pill.

It wasn't my best joke and seeing it written down only confirms that, but at the time it came from a fairly personal frustration that I was having and I wanted to laugh about it with other people in a frivolous way. I hadn't even considered that it could be seen as sexist, because I was only speaking for myself and when I'm onstage talking about my life, I don't think I should have to shoulder the burden of representing nearly half the population.

However, according to my friend, his date was offended by it, claiming that I was undervaluing the gift of motherhood and making a mockery of women's fertility. I know in my heart that I would never do that intentionally, and in my mind the joke was not about that at all, but that's how she felt and there was nothing I could do about that.

Except I couldn't stop thinking about it. I became obsessed with the idea of sharing my thought process behind the writing of the joke with her. I hated the idea of someone walking around thinking that I was a sexist. I hated it so much, I had to get in touch with her just so we could get a coffee and I could sit her down and explain to her that she was a stupid bitch.

Thanks to Stevie Nicks for providing me with the excuse I needed to write this story. I hope that girl sees this.

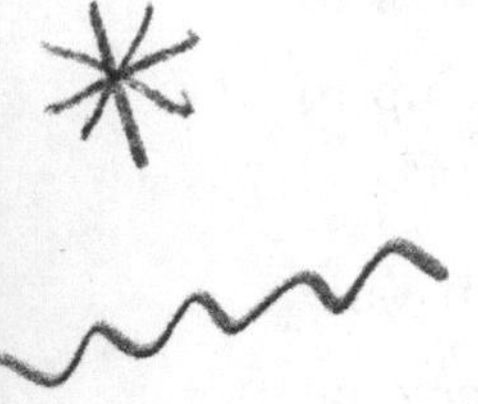

Jacinta Allen

In 2015, my friend Tom told me he was about to try this experiment he'd heard about. He was going to unfollow all his Facebook friends, to help him stop scrolling through Facebook so much.

The idea was that you could still keep Facebook for the things it was useful for, like replying to invitations or messaging people, but your feed would be completely blank. There was no reason, therefore, to waste hours looking through updates and photos and opinions from people you barely know called Brett who you'd met once and didn't even like.

It sounded promising, so I decided to try it for myself. The process of manually unfollowing everyone took a fair bit of effort – it probably took around two weeks to get through everyone – but eventually I had a completely blank feed. I wasn't able to scroll down, even if I wanted to.

For a couple of months, it worked. I was free from endless scrolling and found myself not going on Facebook every day because there wasn't really anything to see. I felt lighter, happier. I had more time to do the things I wanted to do, like stare at a wall or blame my parents for how I turned out.

Gradually, though, I noticed that whenever I saw friends or acquaintances in real life, their smiles seemed a bit strained and their eyes seemed to be searching for something in mine. It took me a while, but eventually I figured out what was happening after a friend of a friend barely spoke to me all night at a party.

Later, I went onto her Facebook page and saw that she'd announced her engagement. A mutual friend had told me the news before I saw her at the party and I thought it was enough to congratulate her in person with genuine warmth and sincerity, but I was wrong.

I started checking out more people's Facebook pages and saw the same thing: announcements of all types being celebrated by our social circle, with no likes from me or Tom.

From that point, whenever I noticed people being cold to me in real life, I'd launch straight into an explanation of my Facebook experiment, telling them in light, happy tones that I'd unfollowed *everyone*, including my family and best friends. I'd even follow up by saying something like, 'I'm scared that some people might think I don't like them because I'm not liking their posts!'

And just as I predicted, people's eyes softened, they seemed generally more relaxed around me and even started laughing at my jokes again.

I had always suspected that people had a bit of a subconscious checklist of who liked and commented on their online posts, and now my suspicions had been confirmed. What seems like a casual like to me is the way some people mentally ease their social anxieties.

Knowing this, I had to make the decision whether I wanted to spend every future conversation at a party breathlessly letting people know about the experiment and telling them to not be offended if I hadn't been liking their posts, or to just give in and get back on the Facebook bandwagon like everyone else. Tom had also noticed these real-world ramifications and so, after many conversations weighing up the pros and cons of what we'd done, in the end, we both chose to give in. Not only did I have to spend another couple of weeks following all my friends again, but I was also spending far more time on Facebook than I had before the experiment.

This wasn't the only online experiment Tom had tried that had real-world complications. Around the same time as the Facebook experiment, he'd begun mucking around with one of those bots you can buy that supposedly get you more Instagram followers. It works by following people and liking their posts and even commenting generic phrases like 'wow' or 'amazing' on your friends' photos. Then it finds out who your friends follow and starts following *them* and liking *their* random posts. Those people may then see you following their account and liking their posts and follow you back, therefore gaining you more followers. As well as wanting to broaden his numbers of followers, Tom also claimed purchasing the bot was an intellectual exercise, as he was just interested to see what it could do.

The problem was the bot had no sentience, so it didn't really understand who were the right and wrong people to follow. The erratic nature of the bot meant Tom ended up following a fifteen-year-old girl who was the much younger sister of a work colleague. Unbeknownst to him, the bot started liking all her photos, including ones of her and her other teenage friends in their bikinis. That meant that people were talking behind Tom's back, not about how popular he was on Instagram, as he had initially hoped, but about how he might actually be a paedophile.

I loved the bot, though; I used to think of it as a conscious little creature, waiting until Tom was off his phone, then grinning maniacally and thinking, 'Now what shall I do?' and speeding off into the ether to like some photo of a distant friend's second cousin doing blackface.

The bot actually ended up doing me some good. Years ago, I'd had a terrible fight with a friend and we'd stopped talking. Around the time Tom's bot was ruining his life, I got a message from my old friend out of the blue, telling me she'd just moved to Sydney and asking if I wanted to do something together. We met up and it was just like the old days. We never spoke about the fight or why she had decided to contact me after all this time. I am a coward in that way. I don't ever like to apologise, because I'm scared the apology won't be accepted. I never even bring up or acknowledge bad things I've done, even when it's clear the other person has forgiven me, in case I remind them of that bad thing and they decide to take back their forgiveness.

A couple of months later, my friend and I were back to hanging out all the time. One time, I invited Tom and we started telling her about all the havoc his little bot had been causing. She made this funny face, and I knew immediately what she was about to admit. She said that a while ago, Tom's Instagram account had begun following her and incessantly liking her photos, and when she looked at his profile, she saw he was friends with me. She figured I must have told him about her because I had wanted to reconnect, and he was liking her photos as a way of hinting that she should reach out to me. So she did.

Maybe the bot was more sentient than we realised; perhaps it could sense that I had a soft spot for it, so it decided to show me benevolence. But, for me, it was yet another spooky reminder of the power of social media likes and how much they can mean to people.

I went to school with a peculiar girl called Jacinta Allen, who, among her many eccentricities, seemed to be incapable of telling the truth. She was one of those compulsive liars you mostly come across when you're young – the kind who tells lies that are so ridiculous that they actually sometimes get away with it, because how do you even begin to discredit the claim that their dad owns Nike?

While most people eventually grow out of this childish habit, some don't, abetted by the fact that their lies often have no real-world consequences. It must be addictive to tell that first lie and have people believe it – instantly you have earned the attention and status that would come from actually having done the thing you're lying about, with little to no work on your behalf. It must seem like the most obvious life hack in the world.

Whenever I meet an adult that's a compulsive liar, I always feel sorry for them. Why haven't they grown out of the habit or had anyone shame them for it? It's like seeing an adult man on the street sucking on a lollipop, or learning to skateboard – there was a time when that was acceptable, but now, sir, you need to grow up.

The worst thing about compulsive liars is when you *know* what they're saying is made up, yet you're too uncomfortable to call them out on it, so you become complicit in their lie. They've now engaged you in a mutual farce, and you have to go along with the sham.

It's one thing to embellish a story you've told for years, where the facts are perhaps less important than the actual act of storytelling. I know I'd prefer a few lies sprinkled in with a story if it's made better for it. I know a girl who is terrible at telling stories – the whole time you're sitting there listening to her monotonous blow-by-blow account of what happened, all you can think is, *This story could really do with a few lies.*

But it's another thing to lie for no reason at all. I used to know an adult liar like that – this guy wouldn't technically make up *entire* stories, but he would stretch the truth whenever possible. If he stayed up until 3 am, he'd say he was up until 6 am; if he got paid two hundred dollars for something, it became two hundred and fifty in the retelling. It was just little lies that he knew he could get away with, which I suppose isn't all that bad or hurtful to anyone – it's just a bit weird.

Jacinta was a liar, that was for sure, but none of us ever felt comfortable shaming or making fun of her for it, because we weren't sure if she was completely right in the head. At the time, we just diagnosed her as being 'a bit simple', but you're not really supposed to say that sort of thing anymore. I used to describe her as someone that seemed like she might have been held underwater at the local pool for a couple of seconds too long during a game of Marco Polo. Compulsive lying aside, she was a nice-enough girl. I had a few classes with her, as did a couple of my friends, who, like me, never had anything bad to say about her, with the exception of the time she used a mallet to destroy the entire class's dioramas in a fit of rage.

Many years later, while scrolling through Facebook, her name came into my feed. It was a post from her account but written by one of her family members – her sister, I think – letting people know that Jacinta had passed away, suddenly.

I stopped, surprised, and I clicked through to Jacinta's profile, where I saw tributes flooding in from people I went to school with, most of whom I hadn't thought about since Year Nine when I moved schools. Apparently, Jacinta had suffered from a massive heart attack a few days earlier and died right there and then.

I messaged a friend who had gone to the same school and asked if she'd heard about Jacinta Allen. She hadn't. I told her what I had learnt, and we both felt really sad for Jacinta and her family. It's funny how when you're a kid, you think of people like Jacinta as these characters who were a bit weird, and you never think about the fact that one day they'll die. I guess that's the reason kids can, as they say, be so cruel.

Months later, I got a text from the same friend. She told me she had been at the shops the day before, when she walked past a girl who looked a lot like Jacinta Allen. She had nearly kept walking; she said the thought of it actually being Jacinta made her feel sick. But thankfully, she stopped.

'Jacinta?' she called out.

The girl who looked like Jacinta turned around and saw my friend. She made a deranged noise and face, and continued to stare without saying anything.

My friend, realising it was indeed Jacinta, said, 'Jacinta, I thought you were … dead,' which is a sentence most of us can only dream of saying in real life.

Jacinta broke down in tears. My friend tried to comfort her, resisting the urge to pull out her phone and cash in some high-level gossip that would see her stock go up in the group chat.

After Jacinta had finished crying, my friend asked her what was going on. Why was she here in this food court ordering a six-inch Seafood Sensation Subway sandwich when she was supposed to be dead in the ground?

After some encouragement from my friend, who was either being genuinely sympathetic or just trying to seem that way in order to extract every bit of information she could, Jacinta eventually admitted that she had faked her own death. The posts from her account supposedly written by her sister had actually been from her. She had also blocked anyone who might have known she was lying from seeing the post.

When my friend asked why she would do this, Jacinta paused for a while. Then she explained that she kept seeing people she knew posting on Facebook about dead friends or family members and getting all these likes.

'No one ever likes my posts,' she said, before adding, 'I just wanted to know what it was like to get one hundred likes.'

Thanks to Jacinta Allen for the reminder that, if you're going to go to the trouble of faking your own death, don't give it all up for a Seafood Sensation Subway sandwich.

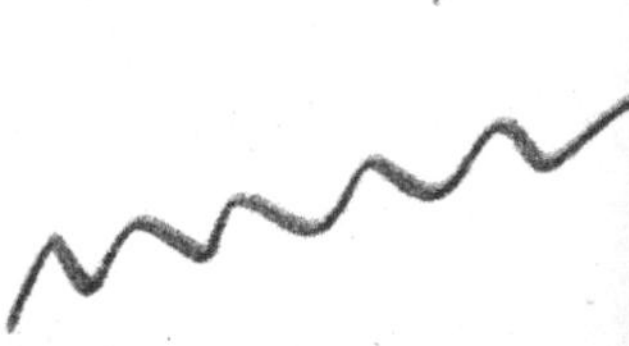

Jeff

My mum used to host these 'jams' when I was a kid, where she and her friends who played in folk bands would sit around our house playing music together. Her two best friends were a married couple who, when they weren't playing folk music, dressed like clowns and toured with the circus most of the year. I thought they were amazing. Jeff was tall and played the fiddle, and Maggie had long hair and played the mandolin, and they were both so nice to me, I felt so special whenever I was around them.

I loved 'doing the rounds' at these jams and being spoken to like an adult, but mostly I loved the fact that my mum would be in such a good mood that she would regularly let out peals of tinkling laughter. When her friends arrived at the front gate of our house, I knew that, for the next while, everything would be fun and nice. Sometimes I have the same feeling when there are people over at my house or when I'm at a party. I just want everyone to have a good time. And it's not for my benefit – when people are having a good time, I don't even want to be there really; I want to go somewhere private and relax, or ideally listen in on them having a good time from the next room.

When my parents' friends came over, there was also the added bonus of a probable treat, which I think is a cornerstone of hope for most kids, even if it's just something small like a cup of tea and a square of chocolate.

Mum and her friends would all sit around and get stoned, playing song after song, which for me was probably the worst part. I liked the bit where they stopped playing and there would be general chitchat and laughter; sometimes when they were singing, it was all too earnest for me. I felt uncomfortable at how emotional they all were mid-song. I still feel that way about some music to this day. I hate the thought of expressing how you feel so ardently and publicly – it is probably my greatest fear. This might sound strange coming from a stand-up comedian, but for me comedy is different. I am never required to actually express my true feelings; if anything, people prefer that I don't.

Occasionally, during these jams, I would be handed a tambourine to bang along to if I promised to do it quietly but, as I got older, I started being entrusted with real instruments like fiddles or guitars. One time, Jeff handed me a mandolin and showed me how to pluck a few basic notes for the upcoming song. I was excited to be given this chance so, as the song began,

I started plucking along softly. I saw a few of the adults look at me approvingly and, when the song finished, they all declared I had a great ear for music.

I loved how easy it was to get a compliment as a kid. I could be speaking for myself here, but I was always very aware at how little effort you were required to put in to get a compliment. That's why the whole concept of show and tell appealed to me so much, because the basic premise was to bring in something that you already owned, or even an interesting stick you found on your way to school, and then the whole class would sit there hanging off your every word. It just seemed so easy. Do little to no work and receive praise and attention? Sign me up.

As I was plucking along to more songs and quickly gaining confidence, I got louder and louder. In my mind, I was now the star of this jam.

After a song where I had played particularly enthusiastically, while people were tuning their instruments and getting up to go to the toilet, Jeff leant over to me and said, in a very kind voice, 'I think for now you should play a bit more quietly. Just until you learn how to do it properly.'

My whole face burnt with embarrassment. I wanted to cry, but instead I nodded really fast and pretended I wanted to go and play with my toys. It was the child's equivalent of 'No, I'm fine. I'm just tired. I might head home. You guys go ahead.'

As embarrassed as I was at the time, I now think what great advice that was. When you're learning something new, watch and learn from others, and shut the fuck up. They should teach that in schools. It is such a gift for someone to tell you when you're being annoying when you're at an age that there's still a chance you can change. Hearing you're annoying as an adult, on the other hand, usually doesn't achieve much except sending you into a manic-depressive episode.

I look back on that exchange as one of the small defining moments in my life that helped me become more aware of the people around me. In that moment, I was making it about myself and being a show-off, and Jeff, probably recognising that he himself had acted that way in the past, let me know where I was going wrong without being rude or hurting my feelings too much. Adults have so many things to teach children; there are so many little behaviours that can develop into more problematic ones if they're not caught and corrected early. If you're lucky, your network of friends and family are able to spot things that might need to be realigned and tell you about it in a kind way.

At age thirty, I went on a family trip. Prior to the trip, I had taken several years off from family events to be an entitled brat pursuing the arts down south. In an effort to prove how good a niece and daughter I really was, I took everyone out for lunch. Thinking the gesture had adequately made up for years of neglect, I relaxed and concentrated on enjoying the rest of the trip, occasionally lending a hand carrying groceries and setting the table.

One afternoon, Aunty Elizabeth, who had taught me how to make cutting remarks and has this way of mocking you while her face maintains plausible deniability, asked me if I could wash the dishes. I was sprawled out on the couch with my hand resting inside a bowl of chips, and I complained loudly over the noise of the TV that I'd done enough on the holiday.

When she asked me what I meant, I foolishly walked into her trap by listing my good deeds in detail.

In a perfect play, she allowed me to go on and on until I'd exhausted myself, then she said in a composed voice, 'Becky, it's been so lovely having you here. We've seen how good you've been with everyone—'

Then she delivered the final blow: '—and it hasn't gone unnoticed.'

I felt so ashamed and grateful to her for that nip, which I needed.

I came back to Sydney and told everyone that story, probably as a way of diluting the embarrassment I had felt and trying to own the narrative. Whatever my reasons were for sharing it, that phrase has become something my friends and I say to each other whenever we feel that the other person is wanting too much praise for something they did, instead of being cool enough to know that the favour will be returned at some point down the track: 'It hasn't gone unnoticed.'

It's a privilege to have people around me who care enough

to keep my behaviour in check, because that means they care about me and how I fit in with other people.

I knew a guy who had grown up in foster care and was a social menace. He was the sort of guy who would smoke your last cigarette or drink your last beer. People didn't like him a lot of the time, but I loved him and still do.

What was interesting was that the same people who didn't like him would claim to be socially progressive, and would happily lecture for hours about 'how important education is' and 'how the system creates criminals because of the lack of housing and mental health funding'. Yet faced with a man who had been shunted from house to house from the age of nine, a man without a mum or dad or any real network of people to monitor the type of man he was becoming, they were unable to extend the same sympathies.

I am guilty of being annoyed by people and the things they do – I've built an entire career on mocking such people. But I think that, deep down, the reason I make fun of people who do things that rub me the wrong way is because the idea that they didn't have someone who loved them enough to gently teach them not to do what they're doing makes me really sad.

So thanks to Jeff for reminding me to not be an annoying little twerp. I shudder to think what I would have been like if I hadn't had that little tap on the shoulder; because, even now, I'm pretty unbearable.

The dead puppies

My parents had a dog called Heidi who was perfectly behaved until she met a dog called Fred who lived a few doors up. She and Fred would run away together all the time. Any time she disappeared, we'd check which dogs were at the pound, and there would be pictures of the two of them smiling side by side.

Eventually, Fred knocked up Heidi and she had eight little puppies. This was a dream for my two younger sisters, Hannah and Charlotte, who were about seven and nine at the time. The puppies used to trot around the house in the cutest little convoy, trying to find places to escape the oppressive Brisbane heat. One of their preferred spots was behind the tyres of my stepmum's car, which was usually parked underneath a shady garage that often had a breeze whipping through it in the afternoons. Because of this, every time anyone had to use the car, we had to do a quick head count to make sure the puppies were safe and sound.

On Christmas Day, my stepmum had invited the whole family over. As usual, she spent much of the day sending Dad off to buy this and that, while my sisters and I kept out of the way so she wouldn't see us and yell at us to do something.

My sisters and I were all lounging around, just out of sight, picking up our Christmas gifts and giving them a shake, then putting them down again, when I heard my stepmum storm into every room of the house, trying to find my dad so she could yell at him for forgetting the butter she needed for the garlic prawns. The heat, combined with the stress of impending guests, meant that any little disruption to her meal planning became a huge deal. She couldn't find him – perhaps my dad had seen how well our hiding technique was working and was doing the same – so, with her face all sweaty and puffed up, I watched through the glass doors as she ran out the door in frustration, jumped in the car, started the engine and quickly reversed as fast as she could out of the driveway.

Then time seemed to slow down.

'Noooooo!' I heard my stepmum cry out in anguish.

My sisters looked into my eyes, and I saw that they realised what must have happened.

I didn't know what to do – I didn't want to see what had happened, but I had to follow my sisters outside because they'd begun screaming at their mum and beating their little fists against the car.

'You killed the puppies! You killed all of them!' they shrieked again and again, repeating themselves until they were hoarse.

Whenever somebody complains about having to hear the same carols on repeat during Christmas, I remember the anguished screams of my sisters and think to myself, *There are worse things one could hear over the holidays.*

My poor stepmum was on her knees, sobbing and begging for forgiveness, as the entire family stood around her. Mothers often talk about the guilt that comes with parenting and look back at the things they did or didn't do, like encouraging their child to play an instrument or working too much, and beat themselves up over it. Usually, I roll my eyes a bit at the things they feel guilty about. Hardly anyone has a perfect childhood. But watching my stepmum on her knees, only ten feet away from puppy gizzards, I realised I was bearing witness to something she would feel guilty about for the rest of her life, and probably with legitimate reason.

Meanwhile, the trauma of the incident was being firmly cemented deep into the recesses of my sisters' brains. It's no doubt still there, lying dormant, waiting until they're in their mid-thirties and hear the sound of a car ignition on Christmas Day, when it will erupt, resulting in them weeping hysterically in a foetal position on the floor.

My dad jumped into action and began grabbing the little dead puppies as quickly as he could and putting them into a bucket away from my sisters, who had just learnt the hard way that sometimes Christmas isn't magical. My stepmum went inside and laid down on the bed to cry for an hour or so, while Dad organised a last-minute funeral for the eight puppies who had lost their lives.

Dad dug a mass grave and placed all of the puppies in it. A few choice words were said about them, which was made hard as my sisters insisted on giving individual eulogies for each puppy and, really, once you've described the attributes of a puppy you've only known for a few days, it's really hard to say something new or interesting about the next one.

Heidi, however, merely seemed a little nonplussed about the whole situation. I felt that if eight of my children had been squished beyond repair in one go, I would be making quite a scene. Heidi just had a sniff around, then went and laid back down on her dog bed with a big sigh, as if she'd been denied a walk or something. I suppose we all grieve in different ways, though she could have at least skipped dinner or let out a yelp.

As each guest arrived in the following hours, they were greeted by news of the mass murder. It was a fairly subdued Christmas dinner to say the least and, due to the upset and drama of the whole day, nobody had bothered to pick up the butter for the garlic prawns. This did not go unnoticed by my uncle, who commented, 'The prawns are a bit dry this year.'

I don't really know why I'm thanking the dead puppies. Maybe I'm just grateful to have a really dark Christmas story, as it makes me seem more interesting at parties.

Brian

I've pissed off quite a few people in charge in my life. The most memorable of them was Brian, the manager of my uncle's spearfishing shop, whom I worked with for about six months when I was twenty-three.

I'd just returned from travelling for a year or so, and had a 'nothing matters' attitude and a misplaced sense that the rest of the world was as open to rejecting hierarchy in a workplace as I was. See, I used to think that people in power responded to playfulness and a down-to-earth approach to things, because that's what I responded to. Whenever I wrote cover letters or resumes, or had job interviews, I would try to impress upon them just how unaffected I was by their power and status. I assumed that sucking up to them would be considered gross and transparent, because that's exactly how I saw it.

Upon my return, my uncle had kindly given me a part-time job working in the warehouse of his store so I could make a bit of money while figuring out what I wanted to do with myself. It was a perfect storm: I was a young, entitled girl who didn't take anyone too seriously, working alongside a man, Brian, who had worked hard to secure a managerial role and who took everything *extremely* seriously.

I found Brian to be very annoying. He had a ponytail that was, in my opinion, far too long and gross. If a ponytail is long enough to be pulled down your back and up through your legs, and there's still enough length left to have it touch your bellybutton, it should be cut off. He was like most managers of small-time businesses, in that he saw workplace decisions as being life or death, and he expected you to be as invested as he was. My uncle, the big boss, loved him because he was such a good worker, and an employer's interest isn't about whether people are having a good time at work but whether the shipments go out on time. But it must have been hard for Brian to be so beloved by the boss, while being detested by everyone else who worked there.

Instead of just accepting that he was a company man the other employees would inevitably dislike, he would try to gain social acceptance by swinging wildly between overly serious pomposity and attempts at being playful and engaging, and he wasn't good at either. He had this habit of forcing you into a conversation you didn't want to be in and refusing to let you reply on autopilot.

He'd saunter up to you, interrupting whatever it was you were doing, and say something like, 'Do you know that seventy per cent of people don't wash their legs?'

'Oh really? That's crazy. Yuck,' I'd murmur disinterestedly.

'I don't think so. We don't eat with our legs, or hug with them, so why should we wash them?' he'd shoot back and I'd convulse with irritation.

You constantly felt like you'd been conversationally backed into a corner. Most of the time I didn't even have an opinion on what he was talking about in the first place – I was merely responding politely in a way I thought would end the conversation quickest. Far from achieving that aim, I'd instead find myself defending something I couldn't have cared less about.

One time, he interrupted my precious lunch break, where I was hiding out behind some boxes scrolling through my phone, just to tell me how much he hated opening up to people. I stared at him blankly while he explained that when he was younger, his dad was really hard on him whenever he showed his emotions. I could sympathise with this, but I also couldn't help but feel that by virtue of telling me this, he was, in fact, opening up. I continued staring blankly while occupying myself with thoughts of how wonderful it would feel to chop off his ponytail.

When I was overseas, my friends and I would play this game where we would walk behind each other and kick the bottom of the other person's shoe, causing them to take a big, unexpected step. As we did this, we'd yell out 'Big step!', which would usually make them and anyone else around us laugh.

On the first day of work, Brian showed me around. This game still fresh in my mind, I decided I would cement my place as the workplace larrikin by 'big-stepping' Brian. As he walked ahead of me to point out where I could eat my lunch, I kicked the bottom of his foot and yelled, 'Big step!' Then I laughed nervously, already sensing that I'd made a mistake.

I was right. Brian did not find this funny. In fact, he let out a dramatic noise and squealed, 'My foot! My foot!'

Looking down, I realised that the foot I had just kicked was wrapped entirely in bandages. He continued to wince in pain as I freaked out and began apologising profusely.

'I just had surgery on that foot,' he spat, annoyed by what I'd done but also, I suspect, by the fact that I'd tried to undermine what was obviously one of his favourite parts of being in charge: walking people around and explaining things to them in a bossy way.

My experiences with Brian made me realise that one of the reasons people in power work so hard to get there is that they actually *enjoy* people sucking up to them. Your transparent desperation when you're trying to get the job or move up the ranks is what these tyrants get off on.

Of course, if you don't value people sucking up to you, as I don't, then you wouldn't crave being a boss, as every day would be a nightmare. But for Brian and others like him, people treating them as though they're special is one of the best perks of the job.

Thank you to Brian for the reminder that if you're going to play a game where you kick the bottom of someone's shoe, just do a quick check to make sure they haven't recently had surgery on their foot.

Mum and Dad

My stepmum always talks about the fact that, from a young age, I was obsessed with whether or not I was going to have kids. This strange quirk is regularly brought up in conversation and, to be honest, I like it when it is. There's something nice about people remembering things that I did when I was younger, as it serves as reassurance that the things I did and said have indeed been seen and heard by people – a relief, as I often feel as though I'm only ever watching other people and that my own personality goes unnoticed.

I do remember talking to my stepmum about having kids a lot from around age six or seven. I would toss up the pros and cons with her, share my fears about how having a child might change my life and prohibit me from doing all the things I wanted to do, and debate whether I would even like my baby.

I still do this now – for example, just the other night, I sat bolt upright in bed worrying about what happens to your phone when you're giving birth. Does a nurse take it from you and put it in a locker? Or is it on a little bench in the birthing room just out of reach but close enough that you might see it light up occasionally? Even more terrifying, what if it never lights up? What if you check your phone after being in labour for sixteen hours and you don't have any notifications? But being thirty-one and talking about birth and motherhood seems more normal to people than being a child who wonders whether having a baby might affect their ability to study further down the track.

My need to constantly discuss procreation as a child was pathological. I couldn't help but bring it up to my stepmum, even when I knew it annoyed her. I'd wander into the room and begin my little spiel about how I loved kids but I was not sure if I'd ever be ready for them. Initially, she'd stop whatever she was doing and indulge me for a while, occasionally nodding her head. But as I went on and on, she would eventually throw her hands up in the air or roll her eyes in a semi-joking way.

'For god's sake!' she'd cry out exasperatedly. 'I didn't think about wanting kids or having babies until I was thirty! Why do you think about it so much? You're seven years old!'

I was baffled by this reaction. I didn't know why I thought about it all the time. I guess I assumed *everyone* was thinking about it. I mean, we all had toy babies and played 'mummies and daddies' at school – wasn't my obsession a logical extension of that?

As an adult looking back, I think the reason I was so interested in discussing whether I would be ready to be a parent was because it was very clear to me that my parents weren't.

I imagine that when a couple falls pregnant, it must feel amazing to know that together you have created something made up of half the person you love. When I was born, everyone decided that I looked exactly like half my mum and half my dad. To this day, whenever someone meets either of my parents, they're astonished at how split down the middle my looks are, and how it's impossible to decide which one I resemble more.

The problem with being half-Mum and half-Dad was that, when my parents decided they didn't love each other anymore, to the point where just the sight of the other person induced rage, I often felt there was half of me that each parent hated. If I smirked like my dad, my mum would growl that I was 'just like my father', and if I raised my eyebrows the way my mum did, my dad would go quiet and look away, clearly annoyed at the uncanny resemblance.

Even now, I get the feeling that people are going to hate half of me. Because of this, whenever I first meet someone, I have this terrible urge to do or say things that are unlikeable. This form of self-sabotage ensures that I know *exactly* what it is someone doesn't like about me, as opposed to having this vague feeling that what they don't like is just, inherently, me.

When I was younger, I didn't understand why people always talked about divorce in movies, because it didn't seem like it was that bad to me. Yes, there was fighting, and I hated being apart from my parents, but I also didn't know what else a family could feel like. Divorce was always presented as a kind of trauma for kids to go through, but at the time I didn't feel like a victim of anything – it was just how things were. I didn't want to be the kid whose parents' divorce made a negative impact on them. I wanted to be a new generation of kid who was so aware and enlightened that I could perfectly rationalise everything that was happening to the point where it wouldn't make much difference in my life at all. And it's easy to see how you would think that when you're a kid, because divorce doesn't affect you as much then. Kids are resilient. It all hits when you're twenty-nine, trying not to bail out of your latest relationship past the two-year mark.

Sometimes, I felt vaguely annoyed at having to pack my bags more than other kids. It never felt completely fair that, of the three of us, I was the one doing all the packing and unpacking and moving around. They would both get irritated at me whenever I forgot anything, like my toothbrush. Looking back, I think they should have been more sympathetic, considering they had both forgotten their wedding vows.

Whatever my parents did, and despite the mistakes they might have made, I'm genuinely thankful for their divorce, especially when I meet people who have had perfect childhoods.

I've seen what a supportive and normal home life can do to someone's personality. Sometimes I'll find myself with someone at a party, not exactly clicking, and I'll finally get around to my favourite topic: childhoods. They'll then reveal their snoozefest of an upbringing and I'll think, *Ah, that's why we don't get along. You've got no neuroses because you were brought up self-assured and happy.* That's genuinely wonderful for them but, excuse me, I must be off now to find someone at this party who is suffering and hates themselves.

In fact, there were a lot of advantages about my parents getting divorced. For one, I got a stepmum, whom I love, and who gave birth to two great half-sisters. I got to be influenced by two very different people with two very different outlooks, and I was able to spend time around all the various people in their respective worlds, and I really owe my parents a lot for that. I did a lot and I saw a lot and it's helped me, I know it.

The disadvantage of having two very different parents, though, was that there was no consistent framework on which to base my personality or opinions; it was all malleable and subject to whomever was around me. A lot of my childhood anxiety was fuelled by trying to please people, and the people I was trying to please the most were my mum and dad.

When you don't have two parents in a good relationship deciding as a team what is best for you, it can be difficult to work out how to act in a given situation. I was in a position where every decision each parent made infuriated the other, so I ended up having to mitigate how mad each one was. As a kid, I became really good at cherry-picking what things to tell each parent in order for them to be in a good mood, which I think has probably helped me as an adult learn how to tailor a story perfectly to the person I'm telling it to. I also think this is what makes me a good gossip. I developed a knack for making whomever I'm with feel like it's me and them against the world. They get it, the others don't, and can you believe what such-and-such did?

I never meant to be manipulative, though I can't say I haven't used these skills to my advantage since then. At the time, though, I just wanted everyone to be happy and for things to be calm. I knew I could say the right things to diffuse the situation, and I knew I could manage everyone's feelings if I worked hard enough at it, but it had the effect of making me very tired. I was always so tired.

When I was twenty-five, I dreamt that my parents were together. I can still remember the whole dream: we were walking along the ocean, near where I grew up, and I felt disappointed. Even though they were acting like they were fine, I could sense that they were both unhappy and I was frustrated that they were pretending to be something they weren't. I wanted them to trust me with the truth. In the dream, I promised them that I would do my best to understand them as people and not think of them as just my parents.

In later years, I've come to realise there was never any pressure on me to fix anything or make it okay. I was lucky to be privy to the inner lives of my mum and dad, who always made their interests and desires very clear. They both showed exceptional bravery in their day-to-day interactions and, while it may have been hard at times when I was young, as I've grown into an adult, it's given me permission to show bravery in mine.

So thanks Mum and Dad for making me, and in the process giving me a unique set of skills and enough trauma to make me a great party guest.

Michael Jackson

A few years ago, my younger sister Hannah begged my dad and stepmum to send her to a religious school. When Dad told me this, I could immediately relate – growing up, I had always wanted to be religious. I thought it was so cool to be forced into conforming to something, which then gave you the opportunity to find ways to subvert or reject it. My mum was spiritual, meaning she did yoga and had a pillow with the word 'dream' on it, but telling my mum I wasn't in the mood to have my tarot cards read to me before bed didn't feel that subversive. My little sister, on the other hand, got suspended within months of enrolling at the religious school because she and a few other girls were caught taking selfies pretending to be Jesus on the cross and posting them online with the caption 'mood'.

The problem with spirituality is that, by the time it reaches the suburbs of Brisbane, any kind of rigidity has been lost along the way. Most of the time, it's just bits and pieces of religions patched together and used to justify people's wishy-washy behaviours and narcissistic tendencies. In the morning, spiritual people are chanting ancient Sanskrit and, by nightfall, they're eating a burger and chips at a chain restaurant that underpays its workers.

I think that I have missed out on something by not being raised religious. I know those religions have snuck in some secrets to life that I'm not privy to, and I'll always resent my friends who bemoan their religious commitments because there's a part of me that suspects they are much better prepared for life than I am, and they don't even realise it.

As a kid, I occasionally went to church with Sophie's family, who were Anglican. On the first trip, I was disappointed to find that the church was not a centuries-old building made from stone, but one of those modern churches that looks more like a council building where you'd go to contest a traffic fine. I also found the sermon a bit of a let-down. I wanted to be made to feel bad by a fiery preacher, to be told I was going to hell unless I pledged allegiance to God. But the pastor was this milquetoast nothing who looked like a JB Hi-Fi employee. 'Just try letting God into your hearts, guys, you know, if it's not too much trouble.' I decided I must be more of a Catholic girl, if I wanted to be shamed and made to feel guilty.

I stayed behind with Sophie after the sermon for youth group, which was even more disappointing. They didn't seem to want to tell us what to do either, and the 'leader' was just some run-of-the-mill horny teenager a couple years older than us, wearing a Stüssy T-shirt one size too small, with bad jeans. He didn't seem to possess any religious authority and, during a game of touch football, used the opportunity to chase the girls around and then pin us to the ground for longer than was necessary.

The closest I ever came to religious fervour was in my devotion to Michael Jackson. Writing this now, I'm finding it hard to find the words to explain how deeply his music spoke to me. I had every album and I knew every lyric. When I pressed 'play' on my cassette player, I felt like I was tapping into something bigger than myself.

Part of the reason I loved Michael so much was because he was like a blank canvas. I could fill in the blanks of information I didn't have. Nowadays, celebrities are so accessible – you can listen to them on podcasts and follow them on social media – and that accessibility makes them seem so much more like us. Michael Jackson was from the era when celebrities were unreal and untouchable, so you could reflect yourself onto them, and they could be whoever you needed them to be. Michael Jackson became this idol onto whom I could project my own belief systems. I really believed in him and I believed anything was possible because of him.

From the age of five, I collected anything to do with him, to the point that, if I saw his name in a newspaper, I'd cut it out and keep it in a scrapbook. I had every version of his face up on my walls, and I became obsessed with learning how to read just so I could properly devour his biographies and any other little snippets of information about him that came my way. He was my escape from the real world when I needed it.

I fantasised about being older and going to his concerts, surrounded by other people who loved him as much as I did. There was a video I had of his 1989 *Bad* concert tour of Europe, which I would watch again and again. My favourite part was when hordes of people ran to the stage as soon as the gates opened, desperate to be the closest they could possibly be to Michael while he was performing. Their faces were so elated and joyful, it seemed religious, while Michael, the solitary figure in front of hundreds of thousands of people, looked like a messiah. I felt like them – like a zealot who would have done anything for this holy man. To this day, on an afternoon resembling the one in that video, when the right combination of breeze, sun and clear blue sky hits me, I get this jolt of happiness that feels like pure worship.

I have never felt fandom to this degree about anything or anyone else ever since. I was so protective of him that I hated it when people made jokes about him, and would defend him bitterly. Even when I spoke to someone who claimed they were a fan, I wanted them to prove how much they loved him, so I could determine whether they were a 'real' fan like I was.

Like a lot of kids, I used to have some minor obsessive-compulsive behaviours. Michael Jackson was my main compulsion. I once had a talking to by a teacher because I couldn't stop drawing him again and again in my notebook, which is probably why I still can't grasp exactly what maths is. I also used to have this little tic where I used my four fingers on each hand, excluding the thumbs, to create patterns of four every time I passed an object or heard a beat. My favourite activity was to listen to Michael Jackson songs and create little finger patterns in time with the song. There were different combinations, but they all had to be repeated on each finger four times, without missing a beat, or I'd have to start again. When I got it right, I'd get this deep sense of satisfaction from having successfully completed a task. Combined with my love of Michael Jackson's music, it would make feel absolutely euphoric, like I was whole.

As well as sending him birthday cards and gifts, I became a member of a few online fan clubs filled with people who were as fanatical as I was. In those groups, people started addressing the many claims of Michael being a paedophile and I started reading all these articles written by people claiming that the victims were money-hungry liars and attention-seekers. I believed them, too; they all seemed to come from reputable sources and were written very persuasively, but most importantly they were saying what I wanted to hear.

This is why I can find compassion for conspiracy theorists – because I know what it feels like to be inundated with information that feels legitimate, even though it's not.

As I got older, my interests broadened and Michael fell by the wayside. His posters on my wall were replaced by ticket stubs of music festivals I'd been to, or Jack Johnson lyrics I'd written on a piece of bark in class – you know, cool stuff like that.

I had also started to think more seriously about the allegations against him, and realising there was perhaps more to them than I had originally thought. When it became clear he was guilty, I felt abandoned, and ashamed that I had defended him for so long. Maybe that's the reason so many religions tell you not to worship false idols. Celebrities are only human after all.

In 2009, when my dad popped his head into my room to tell me Michael Jackson had died, I was upset, but not devastated. It was like hearing the news that somebody I used to be close to had died, but I'd sort of already mourned the end of our relationship.

I was in a bakery the other day where Michael Jackson's music was playing and a woman went up to the counter and asked if it could be turned off. The woman behind the counter began defending him and blaming the media for what had happened to him.

I stood there, paralysed. I felt scared at how easily I could tap into the feelings of the woman defending him. I could see myself saying those same things years ago, but I absolutely knew that she shouldn't be saying them now.

I will say, though, that I believe it's unfair that the burden of responsibility has fallen onto the individual consumer when it comes to a problematic artist's work. That wasn't the first time I've seen someone getting in trouble for listening to Michael Jackson, and here's why I have a problem with it.

Art is often created with one intention, but interpreted completely differently by the people who consume it, which sort of means that once art is out there in the world, it no longer belongs to the artist. When you consume art, it becomes a part of you, whether you like it or not – even if you see a movie you hate, you've still thought about what you didn't like about it, and it's either altered or reinforced your worldview in some way.

Now there are a bunch of people who have Michael Jackson's music as a part of them, and we're being told it's wrong to listen to him and that we have to give that part back.

A lot of the time, these superstars and celebrities get away with acting in terrible ways because the people around them are making money. There are the record labels, the managers, the agents, and the promoters, all taking their cuts of millions of dollars. They don't want their meal ticket to go away, so they turn a blind eye to some truly disgusting and damaging behaviour. Then, once it all comes out, they walk away with their bloated bank accounts and their hands up in the air, claiming they didn't know.

Yet it's the people who bought the albums who are told they can't listen to the music anymore.

It's always the way: the ones who have the most to gain are never the ones who wear the moral responsibility. Fossil fuel companies pump out millions of tonnes of emissions with impunity, but I'm the one who gets a dirty look from the barista when I forget my keep cup.

The whole time Michael Jackson was becoming one of the biggest pop stars in history and the music industry was making millions off his success, we were saving up our pocket money to buy his latest album, and listening to his songs at pivotal moments in our lives or using them to drown out the sounds of our parents fighting. People all over the world, from all different class structures and upbringings, found comfort in his music. It has become inextricably attached to our memories and emotions. He meant something to us. And now we're being told that it's no longer appropriate to listen to him.

Maybe it's not. What he did is unforgivable and my heart breaks for the victims, who deserve eternal love and support. But flawed people will continue to make worthy art – we know this, and we aren't able to stop that from happening. So do we never enjoy anything in case it turns out that the artist we like is bad or evil? Or do we accept that everything we like may be subject to change pending future allegations? I know that, for myself, my experience with Michael Jackson has stopped me from wholeheartedly engaging in anyone's art ever since, and part of me finds that sad. I would hope that in the future there is more responsibility put on the people in power who have so much to gain in the peddling of toxic celebrity culture, and less of a backlash against people who just want to listen to a song from a time when they were happy and blissfully unaware.

So thanks, Michael Jackson. Your music allowed me to experience the religious devotion I craved when I was younger. And thank you for letting me down by turning out to be a paedophile – I can't help but feel that's the closest experience to being religious as I'll ever get.

The gym

The other day I came up with the idea of a household happiness rating – a number in neon lights displayed just outside your house, visible to anyone walking by, that gives a numerical indication of how happy the people in your home are. Would this be good or bad for society? Would I feel better or worse knowing how everyone else was feeling compared to myself? I suppose it would depend. During periods of depression, I sometimes take solace in knowing other people are also feeling bad; I feel more secure being part of a collective. Though if I'm happy and people around me aren't, I'd feel guilty for feeling happy, which might in turn make me feel a bit depressed. If we could suddenly know how happy or sad our neighbours were, would we make the effort to check in more, or would we distance ourselves even further so we didn't have to deal with it?

I think maybe I've always been a bit depressed, and I don't even mean to say that in a depressing way. I'm just saying I think I operate on a base level of depression, so I am very aware of the times when I'm experiencing happiness or joy, which, don't get me wrong, definitely happens often enough for you to not have to worry about me.

It's possible I could just be tired and I've mistaken my fatigue for depression, because I'm often able to rouse myself out of a depressive state by drinking a black coffee. I'm such a tired person. My mum phoned to tell me she thought I might have a thyroid disease, because she noticed that I'm often tired and irritable. I went to the doctor, who told me my thyroid was fine, which meant my mum's phone call was, in retrospect, more just a list of my deficits.

I believe some people are just built with less energy, and I'm one of them. I'm so tired that even if I knew the world was ending tonight, I would still have a nap in the afternoon. I hear friends talking about how they get up at 6 am and I can't understand it, because I know that I have conversations with them at 11 pm at night. The maths doesn't add up for me. Even though seven hours is the recommended amount of sleep we're supposed to have, the idea of that amount of sleep makes me tired.

I don't even have restful sleeps – every time I fall asleep, I'm immediately thrust into intense dreams that involve someone trying to kill me, or me killing someone and needing to dispose of the body. Or I'll dream that I am working a full-time job and, by the time I wake up, I'm exhausted and ready to clock off.

I don't think anyone would consider me to be a typically depressed person, because I try not to show it lest it ruin someone else's day. I deal with depression by making sure everyone is happy enough around me, and once I know everyone around me is okay, then I can have a little depression rest. There have been times when I haven't been completely operational, but hasn't everyone had days like that, and isn't it all so boring to talk about?

My dad doesn't believe in depression. He thinks it can be cured by clearing your throat before beginning a sentence, fussing around with a fishing rod or reading a big book about a man on a ship. It seems to work for him. I admire his mental fortitude. I don't think he's being dismissive of people with depression; he just thinks he's worked out the cure and is only trying to help by sharing.

Like my dad, most people who give advice to people with depression mean well. But it's annoying to be told what to do, and you never believe someone else's advice might work for you. If you're anything like me, you believe your depression is the special incurable kind that only presents itself in people who are secretly geniuses. I can't tell you how many times I was told that exercise might help me to feel better. I'd just roll my eyes and think, *Please, the only thing that can cure this chemical imbalance would be if I had the power to turn people's pets against them whenever I pleased or to ruin someone's life by making them go through an inexplicable rockabilly phase at age thirty-seven.* I wasn't the sort of person who could just start exercising and miraculously turn into the type of girl who listens to the podcast *Serial* and remembers to take her clothes out of the washing machine before they start to smell.

I resisted exercising for years until one day, walking past my local gym, I decided out of nowhere to go in and just see what it was like. The owner showed me around and acted like I was the most important person on earth, so I signed up for a year, and assumed he and I would be friends for life.

I had no idea what to do the first day I went, and the owner who had been so nice to me now seemed a little distant, as though he didn't remember me. Surely I had meant something to him? So I went off on my own and just copied this girl who looked like she knew what she was doing, but it seemed to piss her off. I can completely understand why it would be annoying to have a stranger doing exactly the same thing as you just moments after, but when it's you doing the annoying thing you feel completely justified.

I eventually asked a young girl who worked at the gym if she could show me how to use some of the equipment. The gym is hilarious, you see, because there it's the dumb people who have the power. It's actually wonderful; I find it so relaxing. The girl showed me around with the air of someone who felt sorry for me and all the while I'm thinking, *Don't worry about me. I have a wonderful brain, that's why I'm only just now discovering the gym. I've been able to dine out on my personality this whole time, so please stop cocking your beautiful head to the side in pity every time you look at me.*

She took me over to a machine. To use it, she said, I was supposed to lie on the bench on my belly and pull the heavy part of the machine upwards using my legs.

'It's to avoid getting thutt, you know, thigh butt. Where your thighs turn into your butt. Nobody wants thutt.'

Nobody wants thutt? I thought to myself, *How funny that people don't want this thing I only just learnt about two seconds ago.* I tried to make a quip about how, at the end of the day, we're all there trying to stave off the inevitable march of death. (God, I turn into a complete loser around hot people.)

She stared at me. 'Well, yeah, it's important to keep strengthening your body as you get older, so … let's finish up on this machine over here, then I have to go.' As she said this, she eyed a nearby hunk like, 'Godddd, get me out of here.'

'Yep, cool!' I replied, hating the gym.

Over time, however, I became more confident. I started doing classes and learnt a few basic exercises that helped me at least appear like I knew what I was doing. Plus I did what I always do when I feel insecure, and that's look for other people who are weirder and more annoying than me.

It was then I realised that, due to being blinded by my own insecurity at the gym, I'd failed to notice there were several others who clearly felt the same. Sometimes the secret to feeling better is finding someone a little bit more insecure than yourself, and for me that was a man in his forties who had only just started working out and refused to take off his jeans.

I'm not sure if going to the gym has cured my depression, but I'd be lying if I said I have not found solace inside the big room packed with heavy machines being pushed and pulled by all different bodies. There is a simplicity of walking into a space where there is no other objective except to exercise. It's a great equaliser. No one cares if you're a tortured genius at the gym. Popinjays come in all puffed up from having their egos stroked at work, but, at the gym, no one gives a shit – we just want to know how much longer you're going to be using the machine or if you'd mind moving your towel, thanks. Nobody expects you to be funny; in fact, it would be deeply upsetting if someone tried to make me laugh. It's a place for earnestness and honesty, because we all know why we're there. You can't go to the gym ironically and you can't lift weights as a joke.

I like that about the gym. Yes, it's full of vain people, but at least they're open about their vanity. No one is trying to obscure who they are or what their intentions are, and, to be honest, when it comes to displays of vanity, I'd rather see a man flexing his muscles in the mirror than watch another terrible short film made by a man who insists he's an artist.

Thank you to the gym for raising my serotonin levels to an acceptable level at least two or three times every week – a cherished reminder that sometimes the most basic advice actually works.

Opals

I've always been very defensive of opals. They've come into fashion recently, but, for most of my life, I had people around me saying that they didn't like them – that they were tacky and carried bad luck. I used to storm off and find the opal my dad had given me when I was younger that I kept on my dresser. I'd hold it up to their face, demanding that they explain to me just what was so tacky about it.

'Show me, here, what's so tacky about this bright, multicoloured gem with flecks of sparkle? It looks like the goddamn universe. It's fucking incredible,' I'd say, perhaps a little too aggressively.

And often upon seeing the rock thrust in front of their eyes, they'd fail to explain just what it was that they didn't like about them.

I believe most people have at least one thing in their life they are strangely passionate about and will defend to the death. For example, I have a friend who, three wines to the wind, will without fail bring up the real story behind the myth that each year, you eat eight full-size spiders while you're asleep. As my friend will tell you at length, this is not true. The myth was made up by a university professor as a way of demonstrating to his students how quickly false information can spread.

My strange passion, though, is opals. They are seen by many as common, ugly stones that are easily accessible, when in reality they're much rarer than diamonds. We only believe diamonds are rare because of a widespread marketing campaign that was initiated by the diamond industry, convincing the world that diamonds are the only gemstone that should ever be used for engagement rings. The campaign included ads featuring Hollywood actresses adorned with diamonds. Plus it didn't hurt that De Beers, the largest owner of diamond mines in the world, had a death grip on the market, which meant they could control the availability of diamonds. In fact, diamonds are one of the most common gems in nature. Despite that, the diamond industry continues to be one of the most lucrative in the world.

During the height of diamonds' popularity, the diamond industry started noticing people fawning over this beautiful gem called an 'opal' and, upon hearing about their rarity, they panicked and bought as many as they could. They started giving them to local merchants with the instruction to sell them cheaply and tell stories about how they bring bad luck for some people.Over time, this tactic succeeded in ruining the reputation of an incredibly rare and beautiful gem. People saw them as worthless stones and believed the rumours that they were cursed, which in turn meant they were never revered enough to be put in the same sort of stylish settings as diamonds. Due to their perceived worthlessness, opals were seen by people as ugly. So persistent is this idea that, to this day, my friends, for no reason they could ever articulate to me, don't think much of them.

I'll admit, my own love of opals can be directly linked to how much opals meant to my dad growing up. He used to go fossicking for them in the outback, near Coober Pedy, for weeks at a time, with his dad and an assortment of old men, hoping to strike it rich.

I have a fascination with people who mine for things under the ground. It seems like there's two ways people try to attain beauty in this world: some people are above ground trying to create it from things in front of them, but others are below ground looking to the past to find beauty from what already exists. Mining also seems like such a clash of two different worlds – you've got these gruff manly men looking for these precious stones, which would eventually hang on the necks and ears of women as a way to enhance their femininity.

My dad continued to dabble in the world of opals and, throughout my childhood, strange men would come by the house in their run-down utes with boxes of what looked like regular old rocks in the tray. They'd always be wearing singlets with holes in them – one man's shirt was so threadbare, it had holes all over the front, including right over his nipple. The whole time he and my dad were fondling rocks, turning them over in their rough, calloused hands and spitting on them to reveal the streaks of brilliant colour, all I could do was stare at this man's nipple as it stared defiantly back at me.

It was one of these old blokes who explained to me how opals are made; how, over thousands of years, minerals formed deposits inside the cracks and natural imperfections in rocks. I always felt some kind of comfort in how long it took for beauty to emerge in what was otherwise such a non-event in nature. I used to think the process was so much more dignified and enlightened than the way diamonds are made. Diamonds are made under pressure. That's all. I always felt the process brutish and not interesting, but of course that was my own prejudice.

Now, what I'm about to say may sound corny, but during harder times of my life I have tried to think of myself as an opal. There have been many times when I've felt that there were parts of me that were broken, when situations seemed out of control and spiralled into directions I couldn't foresee. I had times where I believed, and sometimes I still do, that the cracks in my personality went so deep to my core that they were irreparable.

In these moments of self-hatred, I would remind myself of opals. I would tell myself that perhaps these cracks might eventually produce something as beautiful as an opal, something that contains the whole goddamn universe.

So thank you to opals for being undeniably beautiful, no matter how people perceive your worth.

(Book) Acknowledgments

Thank you to my publisher, Helen; my editor, Rachel; and the rest of the team at HarperCollins.

Thanks also to my beautiful manager, Bec, who makes everything happen somehow.